# THE CORPORATE CITIZEN

# THE CORPORATE CITIZEN

## CITIZEN

Governance for all entities

Mervyn E King SC

PENGUIN BOOKS

PENGUIN BOOKS

Published by the Penguin Group
Penguin Books (South Africa) (Pty) Ltd, 24 Sturdee Avenue, Rosebank, Johannesburg 2196, South Africa
Penguin Books Ltd, 80 Strand, London WC2R 0RL, England
Penguin Group (USA) Inc, 375 Hudson Street, New York, New York 10014, USA
Penguin Group (Canada), 90 Eglinton Avenue East, Suite 700, Toronto, Ontario, Canada M4P 2Y3 (a division of Pearson Penguin Canada Inc)
Penguin Ireland, 25 St Stephen's Green, Dublin 2, Ireland (a division of Penguin Books Ltd)
Penguin Group (Australia), 250 Camberwell Road, Camberwell, Victoria 3124, Australia (a division of Pearson Australia Group Pty Ltd)
Penguin Books India Pvt Ltd, 11 Community Centre, Panchsheel Park, New Delhi – 110 017, India
Penguin Group (NZ), Cnr Rosedale and Airborne Roads, Albany, Auckland 1310, New Zealand (a division of Pearson New Zealand Ltd)

Penguin Books (South Africa) (Pty) Ltd, Registered Offices:
24 Sturdee Avenue, Rosebank, Johannesburg 2196, South Africa

www.penguinbooks.co.za

First published by Penguin Books (South Africa) (Pty) Ltd 2006

ISBN 0 143 02508 2

Typeset by CJH Design on 11/13 pt Century
Cover design Flame Design, Cape Town
Printed and bound by Interpak Books, Pietermaritzburg

# Contents

# Foreword

*The Corporate Citizen* stands out from the by now considerable literature on corporate governance for a number of important reasons. In the first place Mervyn King's record of experience in the field of governance is exemplary. He chaired the South African Committee on Corporate Governance, which is named after him. The Committee's two reports broke new ground in terms of their scope, which encompassed the whole range of economic activity in the country, and in terms of their external influence. As a consequence, his advice on matters of governance has been sought by committees and institutions around the world.

As significant as the authority with which he writes is his assessment of the direction which corporate governance has increasingly been taking and the need for it to return closer to its original character and aims. As he points out, the object at the outset was to improve the quality of the leadership which boards were giving to their businesses. Corporate boards were looking for a lead over the nature of their responsibilities and over the standards of accountability and performance which were expected of them. National codes of best practice were published which set out governance guidelines to assist boards to meet these standards, while recognising the diversity of corporate forms. Boards did not have to comply slavishly with such guidelines; instead they were to follow them in ways which made sense in their particular circumstances. It was their responsibility to disclose how far they complied with the guidelines and to explain areas of non-compliance. This 'comply or explain' approach left compliance itself resting, where it should, with the market. It was for boards to satisfy their stakeholders with the manner in which they directed their enterprises, not some external authority.

In effect, the responsibility for raising governance standards lay primarily with boards and with those who funded them, both boards and their funders having a clear incentive to foster that improvement. Their responsibilities in the matter are, however, being eroded by the increasing weight of regulation. The more a rule mentality takes hold, the more complying with the rules becomes the objective, with form replacing substance. As

Mervyn King explains, what began as an endeavour to improve the quality of governance of companies has too often become a matter of compliance – quantitative rather than qualitative.

This brings us to the heart of the matter which is how best to return to that original endeavour of improving the quality of governance. The book's aim is to assist directors to understand what good governance requires of them. Good governance is summed up as involving, *'fairness, accountability, responsibility and transparency on a foundation of intellectual honesty'* and against that background, it is for directors to arrive at decisions which are objectively in the best interests of their companies.

In arriving at their decisions, directors have to thoroughly understand their duties of good faith, care, skill and diligence. These are explained graphically and with a welcome degree of clarity. The book's advice to directors and boards is practical, down-to-earth and grounded in the breadth of the author's experience. It is formulated in terms of the questions which boards, their committees and above all their individual members should ask themselves in discharging their responsibilities. It is through reflecting on and answering these questions in a spirit of intellectual honesty that we can all learn to raise our sights as directors. The outcome is an invaluable checklist against which directors can measure their effectiveness. The need for boards and directors to evaluate their performance is cogently argued, for without that evaluation there can be no benchmark against which to measure improvement.

*The Corporate Citizen* has the further merit of not confining its guidance to company directors. Institutions of every kind require governing and an understanding of the difference between governance and management. The principles of governance as explained and advocated in this book are universally applicable and will perhaps be especially valuable to organisations which are not exposed to the disciplines of the marketplace.

Mervyn King concludes that the practice of good governance is a journey and not a destination. *The Corporate Citizen* will surely prove a trusted guide on that journey, in addition to promoting some rethinking on the nature of the destination.

Adrian Cadbury
January 2006

# Acknowledgements

This book could not have been written without my forty-odd years as a corporate lawyer, chairman, director, chief executive and consultant to companies. I have sat on boards in the United Kingdom, the European Union and Southern Africa. I have advised and spoken on corporate issues in twenty-seven countries.

To all the people with whom I have interacted, thank you for the opportunities and the experiences.

To all my fellow directors and corporate governance colleagues around the world – thank you for accompanying me on my corporate journey.

I acknowledge the work done by Len Konar (a member of the King Committee on Corporate Governance) on the quantitative checklist contained in Chapter 17 and by the KPMG Audit Committee Forum (of which I am a member) on the matters for consideration by an audit committee, attached as Appendix D.

A huge thank you to my assistant Sue Lewis for her hours of careful dedication in finalising my manuscript.

To my wife Liz, a debt of gratitude for her support.

# Introduction

The ordinary meaning of *governance* is 'the manner of directing and controlling the actions and affairs of an entity'. *Government* is the modern word for directing and controlling the affairs of a state and has taken on the meaning of the system of governing a state.

All entities, including schools, charities, clubs, sporting bodies, state-owned enterprises, trusts, associations of persons and incorporated entities such as companies, large or small, need to be governed. Incorporated entities are called companies or corporations. The governance of incorporated entities is generally described as *corporate governance*. Whatever the entity, the principles of quality governance apply equally to all of them.

While we are all governed in the different states in which we live, the question of how we govern the various entities to which we are a party has long been in the byways of our minds. But that time is now past. How we govern the various entities to which we are a party was brought to the highways of our minds in the last two decades of the twentieth century.

This occurred essentially because of corporate scandals which led financial institutions and professional bodies to suggest that guidelines were needed on how companies or corporations should be governed. Consequently, how directors should govern a company was articulated. Since then the phrase *corporate governance* has been loosely used when referring to the governance of any entity.

The various corporate governance codes in operation around the world are different because of the special circumstances in different countries. Originally these codes were all based on suggested procedures or guidelines; in short, they had a *comply or explain* basis. This means that if the board of a company does not comply with a particular guideline, it will explain why it is not doing so and will describe the procedure it has adopted instead.

In some states the government of the day has chosen to make certain processes of governance for companies compulsory by way of legislation. Comply, or else there is a sanction, usually criminal. In both regimes, however, there is a common intent – an endeavour to improve the quality of governance. But what *is* good governance, and can it be achieved on a quantitative basis, compulsorily or not?

I have been privileged to act as a corporate lawyer; give judgments on corporate issues as a High Court judge; act as an arbitrator and mediator in corporate disputes; been a chairman, director, chief executive of companies; lectured on corporate law and governance and have spoken and advised on corporate governance issues in twenty-seven different countries. I have chaired and been a member of corporate governance committees in America, the United Kingdom, the European Union, Southern Africa and the Far East.

I have drawn on this wealth of experience in writing this book. It was when I was chairman of the board and group chief executive of one of the largest textile groups in the world that I began to realise that it was preferable to separate these two roles – and I did just that. I learned as an outside director about the danger of having only one member of senior management as a member of the board of directors. The risk of asymmetrical knowledge on a board – the executive's direct coalface knowledge of the business compared with the outside director's informed knowledge – was exacerbated by that board structure. I have also learned that rigidity in process dilutes enterprise and consequentially a director's ultimate responsibility: performance.

The practice of good governance is a journey and not a destination. It is a continuous learning process. In this book I share with you what I have learned from my endeavours to practise good governance. While the text deals with the principles of good governance, which are applicable to all entities, the subject is dealt with in the context of the governance of companies – that is, corporate governance.

*A note on usage*: I use the term 'he' to include 'she', and the word 'chairman' to describe the person who is the leader of the board of directors.

# 1

# The History and Context of Modern Governance

In the early part of the seventeenth century Amsterdam was perhaps the financial centre of the world. It was there that the great Dutch East India Company carried on its business which stretched around the world. Even in those early days, when the providers of capital were a loose association of persons, complaints were made of mismanagement, insider trading, excessive remuneration for managers, and the lack of disclosure.

Notwithstanding these important issues in this great commercial venture, the question of how one governs such a venture, be it an association of persons or an incorporated entity, was not articulated. It is interesting to note that universally there is nothing in corporate legislation as to how directors should govern. The articulation of how directors should govern companies only commenced in the last half of the twentieth century.

This is even more startling when it is remembered that the modern company, as we know it, started in 1855. Since that time entrepreneurs have been able to implement their business ideas with the protection of limited liability.

During the nineteenth and twentieth centuries incorporated entities prospered with the thrust of the industrial revolution and under the protection of limited liability. The entrepreneurs of that time who, through their families, controlled the equity of these companies, adopted an approach of focusing exclusively on one bottom line, namely the profit one. They did this to the exclusion of all other stakeholders, notwithstanding their being linked to the company as a result of its activities. This exclusive approach to governance meant that the company was directed to improve the lot of the providers of capital, the shareholders, to the exclusion of the other stakeholders.

These wealthy families became the great owners of the equity of their companies up to the end of the

Second World War. Thereafter, financial institutions became the major shareholders of these companies, which by then were listed on exchanges around the world. The financial institutions, however, were and are nothing more than conduits for the persons in the street who, for example, contribute to pension funds which are administered by these institutions which, additionally, manage policies and annuities bought by such persons. Consequently, there has been a shareholder revolution so that stakeholders, such as employees, are indirectly today's ultimate shareholders of the great companies around the world. There has also been a fusion between *stakeholders* and *shareholders* in the sense that stakeholders, other than shareholders, have become shareholders, as well as being suppliers, employees or other stakeholders. Today many employees of a company acquire shares in their employer company.

In the last two decades of the twentieth century questions were asked in America and the United Kingdom as to whether directors were governing Anglo-American companies correctly. These questions arose because it appeared that Far Eastern companies were starting to outperform their Anglo-American competitors. The form of governance in the East was different from that of the West. In the Anglo-American countries the unitary board system prevailed and there were few appointments to boards which could be labelled as representative of stakeholders, such as bankers and suppliers to the company. The opposite was the case in the Far East. At the same time there were great corporate scandals in the United Kingdom, such as the BCCI Bank and the Maxwell sagas. All this led to the formation of a committee in the United Kingdom, under the chairmanship of Adrian Cadbury, which was mandated to produce a code focusing on the financial aspects of governance.

In 1992 South Africa was moving from a situation of discrimination to one of equal opportunity. The majority of its citizens had been discriminated against by not being able to participate freely in the mainstream of the economy. This was to change overnight. There were special circumstances in South Africa – such as previously disadvantaged citizens moving into the economy, equal opportunity rather than discriminatory advantages, and the need for affirmative action. Consequently, a committee, which became known as the King Committee, was formed in order to write a corporate governance code for South Africa. Its remit was wider than that of the Cadbury Committee and embraced issues other than the financial aspects of governance.

The King Committee issued its first report in 1994. It highlighted the fact that companies do not operate in a vacuum. They are a link which brings their stakeholders into an interactive situation.

Certainly, in the context of the new South Africa, it would have been an act of commercial folly for directors to have directed their companies on an exclusive basis, thereby ignoring all stakeholders other than the providers of capital. At the same time a director could not move away from the principle of acting in the best interests of the company. What was recommended was that in directing a company decisions had to be made in the best interests of the company, but at the same time it had to be ensured that the decisions made would result in the company being seen to be acting responsibly towards and responsively to its stakeholders.

Honesty in dealing as an agent for a principal is an immutable principle. While it is true that a leader of any entity, such as a director of a company, is not strictly an agent acting for a principal, he does make decisions on behalf of that entity. In that context, intellectual honesty in acting on behalf of the entity is immutable and non-negotiable.

Governance is a dynamic activity. Governance processes could be and have been affected by events such as swings in the economy of a country, vagaries in an industry, the information communication technology revolution and the United Nations declaration of human rights. One of the consequences of real time information and the human rights declaration is that the exploitation of the employee stakeholder, as in sweat shops, if not a thing of the past is certainly disclosed internationally within the hour of discovering it. We also now live in a world where the way in which decisions impact on the environment is closely monitored by the state, ecologists and the company's own stakeholders. Legislation aside, a director cannot today ignore ecological factors in making decisions on behalf of a company.

Another factor which influences the way we govern companies is that capital moves across the world without recognising geographic borders because of modern electronic technology. Further, in our lifetimes we have seen companies which have created and destroyed communities. This is evident, for example, in the collapsed textile manufacturing companies in the European Union and the creation of the Silicon Valley on the west coast of America. Another influence is the fact that because stakeholders, if not directly then indirectly, are also equity owners, politicians have taken a new interest in the way entities are governed. When there is a company failure it impacts on their voters.

The result of this changed world is that there has been a huge drive over the last fifteen years, spurred on in certain jurisdictions by corporate scandals, to develop guidelines and to pass laws on how companies should be governed.

When the articulation of governance of companies commenced it was in an endeavour to improve the quality of that governance. Unfortunately, a result of the factors set out above is that governance has become a compliance issue – quantitative rather than qualitative. The question arises: Can a tick box approach to, or a mindless compliance with, governance guidelines or rules create good governance?

# 2

# Intellectual Honesty

Can it be good governance to comply mindlessly with the guidelines in a code or the provisions of a statute? Should the approach to governance be qualitative or quantitative? It cannot be good governance for a compliance officer to report to a board that a company has complied with the code or the rules of governance in the country in which it is registered, without the board applying its mind as to *how* the company should be governed. The board has to apply its collective mind to what are the best governance processes for its decisions on many issues.

In Commonwealth and European Union countries

the approach is one of *comply or explain*. The codes in these various countries have suggested guidelines on how to govern a company. If the directors of a company registered in any one of these countries find for good reason that a particular governance process is not in the interests of the business of that company and decide to adopt an alternative process, they should explain why they have adopted the alternative process and why they believe that this alternative process (rather than the guideline) is in the better interests of the company. Where there is a *comply or else* regime, in other words where the guideline has become a rule by way of legislation, there is no room for the flexibility of adopting another process even if it is in the better interests of the company.

In a comply or else regime the sanction is usually a criminal one with oversight by a regulator. The ultimate compliance officer, however, is the market-place – the stakeholders linked to the company. A compliance officer in a company would do a quantitative tick box check on whether guidelines or rules have been adopted. In a comply or explain regime the stakeholders of a company will soon let the directors and senior management know whether or not they agree with the process adopted and the reasons for departing from the guideline. They will either continue to support the company by continuing to hold their equity, to supply the company, to be employed by the company; or, if they believe that the alternative process amounts to bad governance, they will flee it by selling their equity, quitting their employment and stopping supplies. The consequence of bad governance, be it as a result of dishonesty, negligence or unacceptable process, is that stakeholders' support for the company dwindles.

A further issue that needs to be acknowledged is that every director or executive of a company is a human being and subject, therefore, to human frailty. He is not a recording machine. He comes to the decision-making table with past prejudices and present needs. Simply by being aware that one has a duty to practise quality governance, as opposed to adopting a mindless quantitative approach, would start one on the road to becoming a better director.

Enron had all the trappings of good governance. If the shareholders of Enron had looked into the company they would have seen that it had a preponderance of outside directors with good board attendance and board committees such as audit and remuneration committees. So with this quantitative approach the average shareholder would have drawn the conclusion that the company was being well governed. In fact, we now know that it was dysfunctional because of the corporate sin of self-interest.

Special purpose entities had been formed between

which assets were sold and profits created. Complicated structured financial transactions were entered into so that the legal and accounting conclusions could be drawn that the money raised could be kept off the balance sheet. Of course, all this energy did result in the share price being maintained and share options being fruitfully exercised. One can feel the kind of intellectual energy that was employed over years to do all this, but was it employed in the best interests of Enron?

Good governance will not result from a mindless quantitative compliance with a governance code or rules. Good governance involves fairness, accountability, responsibility and transparency on a foundation of intellectual honesty. One has to employ one's practised abilities and honestly apply one's mind in an unfettered and unbiased manner in making a decision that is in the best interests of the company.

The purpose of this book is to assist directors to practise good governance. In the chapters that follow the distinction will be drawn between process and enterprise; the duties of a director acting for an incapacitated entity will be detailed; the governance milieu in which directors act in the twenty-first century will be outlined; the concepts of intellectual honesty and naivety will be detailed; the inclusive approach as opposed to the exclusive one will be expanded; questions will be formulated to be silently asked by a director when sitting at the boardroom table; human frailty will be discussed; the importance of obtaining assurance on the quality of information furnished to the board will be underlined; how to attain this assurance will be discussed; attention will be drawn to IT governance and a checklist will be provided as an aide to improve governance processes.

# 3

# Process and Enterprise

An incorporated company has no mind of its own. This is equally applicable to any entity, such as a school committee. Once a company is registered in a country it becomes a person in law and effectively becomes a citizen of that country as much as a natural person born in that country. Technically a company is immortal, but it is inanimate until directors are appointed. A company is sovereign in the sense that it is the sole owner of its assets and is separate from its stakeholders, be they the providers of its capital or otherwise.

Shareholders have rights by way of contract in terms of the articles or constitution of the company and the legislation of the country in which the company is registered. Shareholders are loosely referred to as the owners of a company when in fact the company is sovereign and is not owned by anyone. The majority of shareholders through their contractual and statutory rights can, for example, appoint new directors or change the very object for which the company was formed, but that does not give it ownership of this intangible statutory 'person'. Assets acquired by the capital provided to the company by shareholders, money borrowed by the company or profits arising out of its business activities, are the property of the company alone.

The standard definition of corporate governance is *the way in which companies are directed and controlled*. A more informed definition would be *processes to help directors discharge and be seen to be discharging their responsibilities created by their duties*. This definition applies equally to all entities which are governed.

Outsiders looking into any company judge the quality of the governance of that company on a quantitative basis. They tick, for example, that the company has a preponderance of outside (non-executive) directors, and not only inside (executive) directors who also manage the business of the company on a day-to-day basis.

Governance is about process, while enterprise involves business judgement calls made for reward commensurate with the risk taken. The governance aspect is determined by how the company is led. The providers of capital accept that acquiring equity in a company involves greater risk than, for example, money deposited in a bank. While the reward is expected to be much higher, it is accepted that the wrong business judgement call might result in a lower reward than a risk-free investment, no reward at all, or the loss of the capital provided.

Consequently, investors in the equity of a company accept that directors can, and probably will, make a wrong business judgement call over a period of time. What they will not accept, however, is that in making that wrong business judgement call the directors have adopted an inappropriate process in arriving at their decision. It is possible for directors to practise bad governance but make a good business judgement call and have a good financial outcome. This may result in some stakeholders drawing the conclusion that the directors are good directors. The converse also occurs – good governance but a bad business judgement call amounts in the eyes of some, quite erroneously, to bad governance. But directors who do not practise good governance *and* make the wrong business judgement call will find they have a disastrous situation on their hands.

For this reason alone it is essential that directors

practise good governance. None of us can get it right all the time when making business judgement calls. None of us is prescient and therefore none of us will always make the correct business judgement calls. Directors or leaders of any entity will, from time to time, even on an honest application of mind, make a wrong judgement call.

From a process point of view, the 'milieu' in which directors have to practise good governance is a complicated one.

Firstly, one is dealing with human beings and consequently with human frailty. Secondly, the licence to operate has become complicated. There are many more licensors for the manufacture of tables (for example) than simply obtaining a licence from the local authority in the area in which the entrepreneur wants to commence his business. He has to consider industry standards, social and environmental issues, investigative media, regulators, etc. Thirdly, the framework in which a company operates today involves not only the local community but the national and, more often than not with globalisation, the international community.

At the same time the board has to act responsibly towards the company's stakeholders. Every company has internal and external stakeholders. The internal stakeholders are, for example, employees, customers, lenders of money, the providers of capital, suppliers, etc, while the external stakeholders are trade unions, local, national and international communities, trade associations, investigative media, stock exchanges, Inland Revenue, political opinion, pressure groups, industry standards, and so on.

A good director identifies where his company is situated in the context of the local, national and international community. He will also ask himself how the company relates to these communities, and where it fits in when it comes to the laws, regulations and mores of these communities.

A board should identify the stakeholders who are effectively the licensors of the business of the company. Today, the licensor of a business is not only the regulator who grants the company the licence to operate its business. There are always other licensors – for example, standard-setting or industry bodies; the media; the individual stakeholders linked to the company through its business such as its customers, employees, suppliers, pressure groups, public opinion makers, politicians, etc. Any one of these licensors could impact positively or negatively on a business and will definitely be needed when the inevitable downturn is being corrected. Consequently, they must be identified and a board should be mindful of them in developing and finalising a strategic business plan. They should also not be overlooked in monitoring how management is implementing the plan.

One cannot practise good governance without identifying the framework in which the company operates and the licensors who permit it to operate. Having identified these licensors, relationships must be built with them because when a downturn in the operation occurs, it is these licensors who will assist the board to correct the situation more quickly.

Appendix A (page 133) contains a graphic of the framework in which a company operates today.

A board can no longer make business judgement calls exclusively with the single bottom line of profit in mind. In making business judgement calls a board has to ensure that they are made not only in the best interests of the company, but that the company will be seen to be acting responsively to and responsibly towards its stakeholders.

As if all the above were not enough, the corporate devil is ever present because of human frailty. Directors have to be aware of the five corporate sins of

- self-interest
- self-concern

- focusing on processes (administration) rather than enterprise
- pride, when a decision has been made which turns out to be the incorrect one and the board is slow to correct it
- arrogance, when the board believes that it has the right formula for its business, its competitors do not, and nothing will go wrong!

There are many laws and regulations with which every company has to comply in carrying on its enterprise. At the same time the communities in which the company operates expect it to act as a decent citizen.

It is precisely because one cannot be prescient that from a governance perspective a comply or explain regime is preferable to a comply or else regime. Where there is rigidity in process a dilution in enterprise occurs. There are many American directors who complain about the cost of compliance with the American Sarbanes-Oxley legislation on governance and believe that the rigidity and stringency of that legislation is stifling enterprise. For example, to acquire the equity of another company listed on the New York Stock Exchange, the CEO of the acquirer would have to certify at some time after the acquisition the correctness of the financial information on a consolidated basis. If he is unsure about how the acquiring business has been operating, the acquisition of the equity of the other company could result in his either not being able to so certify, or certifying at the risk of being imprisoned. Consequently, a tendency will develop to abandon the acquisition of equity and rather acquire assets. This in turn will lead to complicated issues of cession of existing rights and the delegation of existing obligations.

The comply or else regime also negates the intellectually honest approach of directors applying their minds as to what is the best process for the business of the company or for a particular transaction. It cannot be that a single process will always be the best process for every imaginable business or business transaction in the world.

What is developing around the world is a sort of hybrid system of governance where some processes have become compulsory, while others take the form of guidelines, leaving it to directors to explain the alternative process if the guideline is not followed.

Whether the governance regime is one of compulsion or not, its purpose is an endeavour to ensure that directors discharge their duties and practise good governance.

# 4

# The Inclusive Approach

Great entrepreneurs of the nineteenth and early twentieth centuries ran companies for the benefit solely of the providers of capital and had a single bottom line approach, namely, the profit bottom line. In the latter half of the twentieth century people became more aware of the world's ecological problems with the result that throughout the world social, health and environmental legislation was developed.

In most jurisdictions today health and safety regulations apply to a particular business. In running the operational side of a business management has to ensure that it complies with the relevant social, health and environmental legislation.

Today, companies led by citizens in a particular country are themselves seen as citizens of the country in which they are registered. Some of these companies have become more influential in certain countries than the governments of these countries. For example, large multinationals operating in a small developing economy might have gross revenue greater than the country's gross domestic product.

Directors in the twenty-first century have to be seen to be directing companies to be good corporate citizens. The inclusive approach recognises that a company is a link that brings together the various stakeholders relevant to the business of the company. In the modern inclusive approach a board needs to identify

- the company's purpose
- the value drivers of its business, and
- its stakeholders.

This is an important exercise for any entity.

What are the drivers that will create the culture of the entity? The best definition of corporate culture is to think of it as how the representatives of the entity will perform when no one is watching them. The board also needs to identify the stakeholders relevant to the business and develop a mutually beneficial arrangement between the company and the stakeholders. Any strategic business plan needs to combine all these three elements: *purpose*, *value drivers* and *stakeholders*.

Assume, for example, the business of a company is a document and parcel delivery service. The purpose of the business will be easily definable.

The board will discuss the value drivers and identify drivers such as respect for the individual, integrity, etc. But eventually the value driver of reliability will be identified as essential in developing the company's culture. Thus, for example, all employees should ask whether the decision they are about to make will be seen to be a reliable one by the company and will in fact be reliable even though no one is around watching them. Needless to say, a company operating a document and parcel delivery service which was not reliable would not have a successful business. Management will then drive this culture through the company.

In identifying the stakeholders the directors will identify the shareholders, the employees, the suppliers, etc. Among the more important suppliers will be the airline and bus companies. Without the modes of transport they offer, a reliable document and parcel delivery service will not be possible. Having identified this stakeholder as critical to the business, management will be directed to approach the airline and bus companies on a mutually beneficial basis: The more reliably and expeditiously you can deliver our parcels and documents, the more business we will obtain, the more business we will give you, and hence a mutually beneficial arrangement will ensue.

Having done all this, the strategic business plan can be developed, implemented by management and monitored by the board.

In order to practise good governance in the twenty-first century this inclusive approach has to be adopted. In this context, however, a director or a leader of any entity must remember that his ultimate responsibility is performance. Without business success, even the best processes will be hollow.

# 5

# The Duties of Directors of Companies

A director's duties are good faith, care, skill and diligence.

By *good faith* is meant that a director must honestly apply his mind and act in the best interests of the company he is governing. He cannot filch any corporate opportunity for himself and he must ensure that there is no conflict between his interests and those of the company.

The duty of *care* involves acting with that degree of care which would be expected of a reasonable person caring for another's assets. The director has to be a good steward of the company's assets. He should ensure that the company utilises its assets as if they were the assets of his own family, of which he is the head. Acting with care also involves the honest application of mind in making a decision in regard to the enterprise side of the business. When something goes wrong, the question that will be asked is whether the leader acted with care.

In regard to the duty of *skill*, it is expected of each director that whatever his practised ability is, he will apply that ability in the interests of the company he represents. In making a business judgement call, therefore, a director will use his practised ability to add to the debate around the table.

*Diligence* simply connotes that a director must do his homework. A director of a company, or indeed a leader of any entity, who comes to the decision-making table without being fully informed about the issues to be decided there, and who has not studied the information furnished to him in the document pack, is not fulfilling his duties. Diligence also requires that a director understands the issues and the information given to him.

These duties are not usually set out in a statute in terms of which a company is incorporated. They are, however, usually found in statutes dealing with trusteeships or curatorships. The jurisprudence developing the common law duties of directors of companies is approximately 150 years old.

However, the jurisprudence dealing with the curatorship of incapacitated human beings is hundreds of years old.

> If a relative or someone near or dear to you became incapacitated of mind as a result of a motor car accident and you were appointed to look after that unfortunate person for the rest of his life, you would not want your peers, relatives or friends, or the incapacitated person's peers, relatives or friends, to believe that as the individual looking after him, you were actually filching some benefit from his assets for yourself. In short, you would act with the duty of *good faith*; you would ensure that there was no conflict between your interests and the interests of the incapacitated person. You would certainly not seize for yourself any opportunity arising out of your administration of that person's assets.

> Likewise, you would care for that person's assets with the same care you give to your own assets. You would want everyone to see you as a good steward of this unfortunate human being's assets. You would do this to fulfil your duty of *care*.

You would also want to be seen as a person who was actually enhancing and improving the lot of the incapacitated person by applying your practised abilities to improve the person's asset base and consequently his quality of life. In short, you would fulfil the duty of *skill*.

You would do your homework diligently so that you fully understood the incapacitated person's assets and liabilities. If necessary, you would seek advice in order to reach this understanding, but certainly you would ensure one way or another that you understood the person's affairs. In so doing you would fulfil the duty of *diligence*.

In looking after this unfortunate human being you would want to be seen to be a decent citizen. You would do the decent thing for him in every way possible.

A director's duties to a company are similar to those of a person looking after an incapacitated human being. But a company or entity is in fact more incapacitated than our unfortunate human being. It has no heart, mind or soul of its own. Our unfortunate human being still functions (the heart beats) and still has a soul (a reputation). A company once formed becomes a person in law but has no mind, functionality or reputation of its own. It is only when directors are appointed that it acquires a mind, functions and develops a reputation.

Just as no person would want to be seen to be anything other than a decent citizen in administering the affairs of an incapacitated human being, a director should act likewise in fulfilling his duties of good faith, care, skill and diligence for a company. In doing so he also ensures that the company itself is seen as a decent corporate citizen in the community in which it carries on its business.

# 6

# The Relationship between the Company and its Directors

In most jurisdictions today it is regarded as good governance for the chairman of the board and the chief executive officer not to be the same person. Not only is this regarded as good governance, it is also a matter of logic. If it is accepted that a company is sovereign, it has no leader. The chairman is the leader of the board and the chief executive is the leader of the management team which implements the strategy or business plan of the board. The board's function is a reflective one, whereas management's function is an active operational one.

Further, a manager is employed in terms of a

contract with the company as employer. Directors, however, are appointed in terms of the relevant statute of the country. Directors are accountable to the company, whereas the chief executive is usually accountable to the board. It is often loosely said that directors are accountable to the shareholders. In a listed company, for example, the profile of the shareholders can change from day to day. Different shareholders have different goals. Some want increased dividends, whereas others prefer no dividends and an increase in the capital value of their shares. Directors certainly are not accountable to the company's stakeholders but, as has already been pointed out, it is incumbent on directors today, while acting in the best interests of the company, to act responsibly towards and responsively to the stakeholders who are relevant to the business of the company.

A director is a director with all his duties and concomitant responsibilities. In the last few decades of the twentieth century business jargon has classified directors as *executive, non-executive, independent non-executive* and *senior independent non-executive.*

- The executive director is employed by the company and is also a director;
- the non-executive director is not employed by the company but is a director;
- the independent non-executive director is

defined almost universally as one who is not employed by the company, has no contractual link to the company, is not an adviser to the company, is not a shareholder (certainly not a material one) and receives only his fee as a director;

- the senior independent non-executive director is independent and non-executive, but liaises with the major institutional shareholders of the company.

All directors have the same duties and responsibilities unless some specific duty is added by way of contract between the company and a particular director.

While the board has collective authority, each director has individual responsibility. Consequently, if a decision of a board subsequently turns out to have been a bad business judgement call and it is contended that this amounts to a failure in the duty of care, the law looks at the conduct of each director and his own level of experience in deciding whether or not that director is responsible. Every director must be aware that his personal estate is on the line arising out of his appointment and following his conduct as a director, whether by way of commission or omission.

Several commentators prefer to label directors as *insiders* or *outsiders*. The inside directors are those who are employed by the company and are also appointed directors, and outsiders are those who are not employees but are directors.

The constitution of a board is important. It is necessary to know what skills are required around the boardroom table in order to have the appropriate mix for the business of the company. There is usually a mix of coalface knowledge (the inside directors) and outside practised abilities (the outside directors) who, collectively, will hopefully make the best business judgement calls in regard to the company's business. A board that consists wholly of outside directors does not have the helpful interchange of coalface knowledge with outside abilities which a board made up of both inside and outside directors has. While there is no empirical evidence for this, better reflective business judgement calls will probably be made by a board of both insiders and outsiders, with a preponderance of outsiders, compared with a board made up entirely of outside directors.

An executive who is appointed a director should be paid a salary for his management activities and a separate fee for his director's role. His remuneration as director and manager should be separated in the annual report. This is because it is often reported that an executive director's remuneration is exorbitant, whereas he probably attends four two-hour board meetings a year and spends six nights and six days a week carrying out his operational duties as a manager, but not as a director.

Awareness of personal liability and the fact that the role of a director is a reflective decision-making one based on information furnished mainly by management, makes the application of mind by a director more acute. It also drives him to ensure that he understands what is happening at a board meeting when a decision is made.

The role of the chairman of the board is critical in the decision-making process and consequently his role is dealt with separately in the following chapter.

# 7

# The Chairman

A meeting of the leaders of any entity requires a chairman. The chairman must concern himself about the place of the meeting, the timing of the meeting and the contents of the agenda.

Meetings which last more than a few hours are usually unproductive. People lose concentration and minds start to wander. A good chairman will be able to prepare a meeting in such a way that it will finish within two to three hours.

Obviously, the place where the meeting is held is important. Because body language is important, members of the board need to be in a place where they can not only hear each other clearly but can see each other as well. In the twenty-first century the availability of electronic facilities is also relevant.

The essential part of a meeting is the content. This is settled by way of the *agenda*. This document may be drafted by the senior manager of an organisation – in corporate terms, the chief executive, the chief financial officer and/or the company secretary – but the chairman must have input into the finalisation of the agenda.

The chairman needs to prepare for the meeting by ensuring that he has read all the documents carefully, understands them and, in addition, has spent time with senior management prior to the meeting. Again, in corporate terms this means that the chairman should spend time with the chief executive, the company secretary, the financial director and/or the chief information officer to ensure that he has a clear understanding of the objectives of the meeting.

The chairman has constantly to keep in mind that he has the key role of leading the board in discussion, reasoning and decision. Several people have likened the role of the chairman of a meeting to that of the conductor of an orchestra. The conductor of an orchestra, however, has a set script by which he leads the various players in the orchestra, the players read the same script, and they all produce the same harmonious music. In a meeting of people, however, there is no set script. There will be reasoning by persons with different backgrounds, different levels of education, different practised abilities, different levels of knowledge of the business, past prejudices and present needs, and the outcome is uncertain. The only thing that is common to the persons around the table and the chairman is the pack of documents before them – and each board member might have a different understanding of, or different view on, any issue that is to be discussed. The meeting will not necessarily be harmonious, and yet the chairman must try to bring it to a harmonious, unanimous conclusion.

The chairman has to ensure that the board does not get involved in management. He has constantly to remember that the board's role is a reflective one – strategy rather than activity.

A good chairman will get to know the strengths and weaknesses of each person around the boardroom table. He will insist that the pack of documents reaches each member who is to attend the meeting timeously and, further, he will make sure that the information being furnished in the pack is in understandable language. Management tends to develop a jargon for the company's business and uses it without appreciation of the fact that the outside directors may not understand it. It is essential that a chairman ensures that all discussion is directed through him, for he will lose control of the meeting if members around the table talk directly to each other and not through him.

A good chairman is also a good listener. He should be the last person to enter the debate and the last person to express a view on an issue, if he does so at all. He must have the skill to draw the threads of a discussion together so that a fabric is woven of the decision which, when inspected (probably a few years down the line), will show that the directors truly applied their minds to the issue. This may be of significance if the decision turns out to have been a wrong business judgement call.

It is important for the chairman of the board to liaise with the chairmen of every board committee (especially the audit committee) and have an understanding between them in regard to the presentation of any matter with which the respective subcommittee is concerned. It is very important in regard to the presentation of the annual financial statements of the company that the board chairman and the audit committee chairman meet and discuss it in detail.

Perhaps the most difficult skill for the chairman to develop is the ability to recognise that the members around the table have to operate as a team, and yet he needs to encourage creative tension between them so that there is effective debate in the boardroom. Further, while he has to be collegiate, he also has to be at arm's-length because at some time the chairman is going to be called upon to arbitrate an issue, dismiss a senior executive or call on a colleague to resign.

The chairman should try to meet at least twice a year with his outside directors so that a discussion without management present can be held about, inter alia, issues such as the ability of the management team and succession planning. A chairman must also know his rights and duties when chairing a general meeting. He should ensure that the chairmen of subcommittees are present at the annual general meeting.

The chairman has to be aware that he becomes the image of the company. Saying that the fish rots from the head is true about the leaders of any entity, but more particularly of the chairman. He has to be plugged into the politics, the economics and the major issues in any country in which the company carries on its business. In a lot of companies today a chairman has to keep in touch with what is happening internationally as well.

With the question of triple bottom line reporting – social, economic and environmental – becoming a greater issue in the twenty-first century, the chairman has to ensure that the board has identified the non-financial aspects relevant to the company's business and that the company reports on its corporate social investments.

The chairman must endeavour to find ways in which bad news will reach the top more quickly and he must become an expert in asking a critical intellectually naive question when he does intervene in a debate. He must also ensure that:

- at least once every two years the board discusses the purpose, the value drivers and the identity of the stakeholders of the business of the company;
- on an annual basis, the key risk areas involved in the business and the key performance indicators are reassessed, and
- the strategic plans of the business are discussed when necessary.

A chairman needs to know that the members of the board have done their homework. One of the best ways of doing this is, after an issue has been discussed and a vote has been taken, to ask any member of the board to motivate in a reasoned manner why he voted the way he did. If that particular board member has not done his homework or has not understood the issue discussed, it will soon become apparent from the way he motivates why he voted as he did. A chairman need only do this once or twice to ensure that board members do their homework, listen carefully, and ask questions if they do not fully understand the issue being discussed.

# 8

# The Intellectual Naivety of the Outside Director

Intellectual naivety is commonly referred to as 'asking the dumb question'.

An experienced outside director knows that he is not going to understand the business of a company immediately. He may have been in the particular industry for some years, but each company has its own challenges and runs its business in a particular manner. Experienced outside directors know that a period of 'apprenticeship' is required.

Each company or industry develops its own jargon. The strength of the outside director is displayed by asking intellectually naive questions and seeking explanations in clear language free of the jargon of the particular business or industry. The outside director should insist on reports being in understandable language with, if necessary, a glossary of terms being delivered with each board document pack.

The outside director must make sure that he understands the answers to his questions. He should also pay attention to body language when executives or executive directors answer his apparently uninformed questions.

In developing a risk matrix for a company, management often gets lost in detail. The board should focus on those risks which could destroy the company as a competitor in its industry. This is important not only from the negative aspect of risk, but also from the positive side. Risk does not only involve the avoidance of loss. It also involves the understanding of risk to aid in seizing a business opportunity. What are the three major risks which could harm the business of the company and how should they be ranked in importance? Astonishingly, when this question is put to a board with the request that each director put the answer in writing it usually results in quite different answers!

Every company runs the risk of its CEO being

headhunted by a rival company. One of the most important duties of a board is to ensure that there is some succession planning for the senior management; more particularly, the CEO, the chief operating officer, the chief financial officer and the chief information officer. The outside director needs to ask: What are the succession plans in this company?

The board has a duty to endeavour to grow the company's business, which can be done either acquisitively or organically. If there is to be an acquisition, how is the company going to pay for it? Does it have sufficient cash resources? What will the debt/equity ratio be after the acquisition? And if management believes that the year ahead is going to be much improved, the outside director needs to ask what factors will be different in the year to come in order to achieve this.

In a lot of companies debtors are the largest asset on the balance sheet. Consequently, questions should be asked on the quality of the book, the cost of financing the book and about overdue amounts. If there is any litigation in progress, a full explanation should be requested.

The famous case of the President of the New York Stock Exchange and the package that was payable to him on his resignation illustrates that it is no answer for a board to say that the matter of compensation was left to the Remuneration Committee. The committee is there to investigate, to benchmark and to make recommendations on compensation. It is the board which actually has to fix the compensation. A board can delegate certain actions to committees, but it cannot abdicate its responsibilities. So the outside director should ascertain and understand the detail of the remuneration of senior executives. The question of the remuneration of executives has become a matter of concern not only to shareholders but to society generally.

This intellectually naive approach by outside directors assists senior management in obtaining a deeper and better understanding of the company's business. It compels management to focus its mind on issues which are not clearly understood by outside directors.

# 9

# The Silent Questions

As already pointed out, a director's duties are those of good faith, care, skill and diligence.

The duty of good faith is usually tested in court by applying common sense principles. The question that is asked is whether the director has behaved as an honest man of business might be expected to behave in the circumstances of each case. As a court in England pointed out, directors are required to behave 'bona fide in what they consider – not what a court may consider – is in the interests of the company ...' Directors cannot, however, be supine and if the need for enquiry arises they must do so. Thus even if they are not dishonest it can be concluded that they failed to carry out their duty of care. On the other hand, directors are not required to act 'in a vague mood of ideal abstraction from obvious facts which must be present in the mind of any honest and intelligent man when he exercises his powers as a director', per Latham, C.J. in an English case.

Courts have always referred to the heavier duty of good faith and the lighter duties of care, skill and diligence. In the locus classicus of the City Equitable Fire Insurance Company case, Romer, J. said in 1925 that 'a director need not exhibit in the performance of his duties a greater degree of skill than may reasonably be expected from a person of his knowledge and experience'.

Courts in the twenty-first century are applying more objective tests to the duties of skill, care and diligence. For example, in regard to the executive who is elevated to the board, reference will be made to his service contract as an employee of the company. The court will also look as to whether an outside director has any specific mandate in regard to his appointment as a director. Courts have recently said that the statement of Romer, J. applies only to a director's exercise of his duty of skill, and not in regard to his duties of care and diligence. The courts have now expressed the view that the duties of care and diligence should both be looked at objectively. The modern test, therefore, is what a reasonable director who acted honestly, diligently and with skill would have done in the circumstances of each case.

The average director cannot be expected to apply these legal tests in the heat of the boardroom. More particularly is this so when one considers the different aspects of these duties gleaned from American, English and Commonwealth judgments.

The duty of good faith connotes
- reliance,
- trust,
- integrity,
- not acting in conflict with the company,
- not seizing corporate opportunities,
- having one's remuneration as one's only advantage,
- acting in an unfettered manner, and
- acting only in the interests of the company.

The duty of care involves
- serious attention to the matters at hand,
- stewardship,
- transparent communication, and
- protection of the reputation of the company.

The duty of diligence involves
- industry,
- attention, and
- the company's relationships with stakeholders.

The duty of skill is
- a matter of how one evaluates the information furnished to one at the boardroom table, and
- the honest application of one's mind, having regard to one's practised ability, skill and experience, in making a decision on behalf of the company.

How does the average director make sure that he is complying with these duties, let alone understand the tests pertaining to them?

The answer lies in a director silently asking himself ten pertinent questions in regard to the issues before the board. These questions have been developed by the author during the course of his own personal experiences of advising companies and directors over a period of forty years, acting as a director of companies listed on main stock exchanges on three continents, and having regard to numerous judgments and the Business Judgment Rules formulated in America. The questions are designed to help a director to discharge his duties on a qualitative basis. As already pointed out, this is the true test of good governance rather than a mindless quantitative compliance with a code, be it voluntary or compulsory.

*The first question*: 'Do I as a director of this board have any conflict in regard to the issue before the board?' As remote as any conflict might be, disclose it. This disclosure is not an end to the enquiry. The following question should then be asked: 'Should I excuse myself from the remainder of the board meeting or should I make my contribution, having regard to the fact that I was asked to be a member of the board either for my practised ability or because of my representativity?' If the answer to that question is to remain in the boardroom and to make your contribution to the decision-making process, the next question to ask yourself is whether to vote or not. Generally, the common law of every country stipulates that where there is a conflict of interest the director should not vote, but the modern approach, either by statute or by way of a provision in the articles or constitution of the company, is that notwithstanding the conflict on a disclosure of that conflict, a director can vote. This is probably the most difficult issue arising out of this first question. It will be appreciated that one needs to answer all these questions on an intellectually honest basis in order to discharge the duty of good faith.

*The second question*: 'Do I have all the facts to enable me to make a decision on the issue before the board?' Not projections or assumptions, but *facts*. How often are we dazzled by electronic presentations? In the nature of things, particularly in decisions involving capital expenditure, one is dealing with projections or assumptions. A director must separate out facts from projections and assumptions. If he believes that all the facts are *not* before the board and, objectively speaking, there are more facts that can be ascertained, it is his duty to ask for those facts or to request that the meeting be adjourned. A positive answer to this question is absolutely necessary in order to discharge one's duties of care, skill and diligence.

*The third question*: 'Is the decision being made a rational business one based on all the facts available at the time of the board meeting?' Nothing more can be asked of a director. The wisdom of hindsight cannot replace a director's foresight. Notwithstanding this proposition, a court will objectively examine whether the decision was rational at the time. One needs to ask this question more particularly in the context of the best interests of the company. If the decision is not a rational business decision in the interests of the company, then obviously one is not discharging one's duties of good faith and care.

*The fourth question*: 'Is the decision in the best interests of the company?' This seems, on the face of it, an easy question to answer. It is, however, one of the most difficult ones to try to deal with in the boardroom. In the modern world one invariably has conflict which has to be managed. It is *how* it is managed that is important. For example, one might be a shareholder as well as a director and the issue in the boardroom is whether or not dividends should be declared. This is an excellent example of realising that one is acting in the real world and not altruistically or in the abstract. One cannot, however, make a decision which one believes to be in the interests of the major shareholder. The major shareholder is not the company to which the director owes his allegiance. Further, shareholders' interests differ. For example, some shareholders might want capital appreciation, while others might want larger dividends. Also, a company's shareholder profile changes from time to time, more particularly if the company is one listed on an exchange. In the context of this question one has to divorce oneself from the person or organisation who nominated one as a director. It may well be that the decision in the best interests of the company is not in the best interests of the director's nominator. So be it, because to discharge one's duty of good faith one has to make that decision in the best interests of the company even though it might not be in the interests of one's nominator.

*The fifth question*: 'Is the communication of the decision to the stakeholders of the company transparent with substance over form and does it contain all the negative and positive features bound up in that decision?' Transparency is a pillar of good governance. It has a withering effect on misconduct and the more transparent one is in one's communication (without giving away confidential information of the company), the less chance there is of any suggestion of misconduct. A bright light is the best policeman when it comes to governance. There should never be an attempt to create substance by the use of form.

*The sixth question*: 'Will the company be seen as a good corporate citizen as a result of this decision?' This question is necessary because, as already pointed out, a company does not operate in a vacuum. It operates in a community. Consequently a board must envisage how the company will be perceived, arising out of its decision, not only by the local but also by the national community. More often than not these days regard must also be had to the reaction to the decision of the international community. Sustainability is something of which everyone today is aware. The United Nations human rights declaration, social, health and environmental legislation and interest groups, ensure that directors can no longer focus only on the providers of capital and ignore the company's other stakeholders. Here a distinction must be drawn between the duty to account to the company, which is the director's duty, and the fact that the company might actually be called to account by stakeholders by way of tort or statute, for example, for polluting the environment. Development for short-term gain must not be undertaken if it compromises the long-term sustainability of the company and the ability of future generations to meet their own needs. In the modern world it is accepted that ownership creates responsibilities. A company as owner of assets cannot ignore the social, health and environmental impact of that ownership.

*The seventh question*: 'Am I acting as a good steward of the company's assets in making this decision?' This is certainly a decision one would ask as the head of a family if it were one's family's assets. It is an essential question in order to be able to discharge the duty of care.

*The eighth question*: 'Have I exercised the concepts of intellectual honesty and intellectual naivety in acting on behalf of this incapacitated company?' These concepts have been explained in earlier chapters but it is necessary to ask oneself in the boardroom whether one has practised them in the decision-making process.

*The ninth question*: 'Have I understood the material in the board pack and the discussion at the boardroom table?' We are flooded these days with jargon, particularly in the business world. Outside directors do not have the knowledge of the jargon used by insiders in the day-to-day running of the company's business. One needs to ensure that one actually understands the documents in one's board pack and, more particularly, that one understands all the answers to the questions which have been asked at the meeting. If one has not understood, it is one's duty to say so and to seek understanding. If for any reason one believes that a manager or any other person is misinforming one then one cannot remain supine. Having been put on enquiry one must enquire.

*The tenth question*: 'Will the board be embarrassed if its decision and the process employed in arriving at its decision were to appear on the front page of a national newspaper?' Obviously if the answer to any part of this question is in the affirmative one needs to continue addressing the issue before a decision is made. A director cannot discharge his duties if a decision of the board dilutes a company's reputation.

# 10

# Risk and the Non-financial Aspects

As already pointed out, directors have individual liability when something goes wrong. It is to be noted that it is *when* and not *if*, because nothing in corporate life is certain. One is dealing on the enterprise side with uncertain future events and one cannot predict with certainty what is going to happen in the future. Directors, however, have to place themselves in a situation so that they can make the best possible business judgement calls.

Consequently, it is important to obtain assurances of the quality of information coming up to board level. It is in this context that control systems and internal audit processes are so important, particularly to the outside director. A competent internal audit assists directors in discharging their duties and responsibilities.

As business is the undertaking of risk for reward, the identification of risk in a business is essential. Risks take various forms; namely, *strategic*, *operational*, *financial*, *non-financial* and *compliance*.

- Strategic risk occurs in the planning of the business and its future strategy.
- Operational risk is concerned in the day-to-day management of the company.
- Financial risk involves the question as to whether the debt equity ratio, for example, is correct for the conduct of a particular business.
- Non-financial risk revolves around questions of sustainability of the organisation and focuses on health, social and environmental issues relevant to the business.
- Compliance risks are involved in complying with laws and regulations relevant to the business conducted by the company.

Leaders today grapple with the non-financial aspects of risk. Sustainability is an issue that should be considered by every board. *Sustainability* may be defined as development that meets the needs of the present without compromising the ability of future generations to meet their own needs. This definition was developed at the World Summit in Rio de Janeiro in 1992 and confirmed in Johannesburg, South Africa, in 2002.

It is accepted today that ownership creates responsibility. No citizen of a country would want it to be known that he permits noxious gases or noises to escape from his residence to a neighbour's residence. It is generally regarded in society today that companies or any entities which own assets have a similar responsibility to act as decent citizens. Consequently, the triple bottom line of reporting has been developed, embracing social, economic and environmental issues relevant to the business of the company. Directors today have to deal with stakeholder relations, good conduct practices, safety, health and environmental issues, human capital and corporate social responsibility generally.

Another reason for this becoming a corporate necessity today is the merging of the identity of stakeholders. Some employees own shares in the very company in which they work, as do some suppliers who supply the company with goods or services. In short, employees and suppliers are shareholders and vice versa. The result is a merger or fusion of stakeholders.

Then there is also the shareowner revolution which has taken place since the end of the Second World

War. Today it is no longer wealthy families who are the great shareholders of some of the great listed companies. It is the great financial institutions who are the great shareholders of today. These institutional shareholders, however, are merely conduits for all the persons in the street who are contributors to pension funds, unit trusts etc, which are administered by these institutions.

However, all these stakeholders have one common interest with regard to a business, and that is its sustainability. The shareholder who is happy with the capital growth of his shares or his dividends wants to know that the business is a sustainable one. The employee, who has employment and is able to support his family, wants to know that his employment will continue. The suppliers obviously want the company which they supply to continue to be a successful one. Customers want companies that produce good products to continue to do so. The local community in which the company carries on its business, offering men and women in that community the opportunity to improve themselves, also wants the company to be a sustainable one. Even the regulator, who is content that the company is using its best endeavours to comply not only with the letter but with the spirit of regulations, wants the company to be sustainable.

One of the most interesting cases on the importance

of the non-financial aspects of a business is that of Talisman Energy, a company listed on the Toronto Stock Exchange. The business of this company was to search for, drill, find oil and refine it. It went to the Sudan and found oil. In the course of doing so it employed many people, created livelihoods for those people and improved the infrastructure of the region.

At the same time a civil war broke out in the Sudan which was characterised as being a Christian/Muslim conflict. In Canada and the United States, which are in the main Christian countries, non-governmental organisations and churches started demanding that Talisman Energy should withdraw from the Sudan. Their annual general meetings became chaotic and the share price plummeted on the Toronto Stock Exchange.

Talisman Energy eventually obtained third party advisers to record on a verification basis the good that they were doing in the Sudan – such as improving the infrastructure, creating livelihoods for the local people, etc. Eventually, over a period of a few years the calls for the company to leave the Sudan subsided and the share price recovered. This is a real example of how important non-financial aspects can become in the life of a company.

# 11

# Internal Audit

Serving as a member of a board of directors involves risk. This risk is accentuated because of the problem of asymmetrical knowledge at board level. As explained earlier, this is the different level of knowledge of the day-to-day running of the business of the company which the inside executive director possesses, but which the outside non-executive director does not.

Sometimes statements involving the business are not accurate or comprehensive enough for there to be a proper understanding by the outside director. While the outside director can rely on the statements of the executive director, if he has any reason to enquire, he should do so. Further, he should endeavour to obtain what assurance he can as to the quality of the information at board level. One of the most important tools of assurance is that of internal audit. The other assurances come from management, independent external audit and the audit committee.

The Institute of Internal Auditors defines *internal audit* as an 'independent objective assurance and consulting activity designed to add value and improve an organisation's operations. It helps an organisation accomplish its objectives by bringing a systematic, disciplined approach to evaluate and improve the effectiveness of risk management, control and governance processes'.

The internal audit team may consist either of employees of the company or outsiders can be appointed. Regardless of whether it is the one or the other, the internal audit team has to have status in the company. This is usually achieved by the head of the internal audit team having access not only to the chairman of the audit committee but also, if necessary, to the chairman of the board. The head of the internal audit team should attend all meetings of the audit committee. The internal audit team must develop its internal audit plan, together with the external auditors, to ensure that there is no overlapping of work.

The importance of internal audit is such that the appointment of the head of internal audit should not be made, and nor should he be dismissed, without the concurrence of the audit committee.

The internal audit team needs to establish its credibility in regard to the quality of its work so that the external auditor can place reliance on this work. This assists in the expedition of the external audit and also can reduce the costs of the external audit.

The outside director cannot test the reliability and integrity of systems in the company. Notwithstanding, in most jurisdictions today it is expected of a board to make a statement on the adequacy of internal controls of the company and confirm that they are designed to provide reasonable assurance as to the integrity and reliability of the financial statements as well as to safeguard the company's assets.

There should be a clear segregation of duties between the internal auditor and any other part of management. This is particularly important because directors need an assurance from internal audit that there has been no material breakdown in the functioning of the controls, procedures and systems of the business of the company.

In most jurisdictions today the external auditor is

expected to concur with the statement by directors that the internal controls are operative and can be relied on in regard to the quality of the financial statements. Obviously, if the external auditor cannot concur, he needs to identify the problems in the controls or processes.

In any company which does not have an internal audit the risks for the outside director are increased. It is one of the most important assurances of the quality of the information on which the outside director acts.

Operationally, the head of internal audit should report to the chief executive officer but have a dotted line function to the chairman of the audit committee and, if necessary, to the chairman of the board.

An effective internal audit function should include a review of the reliability and integrity of the financial and operating information and the means used to identify, measure, classify and report such information. Compliance with policies, plans, procedures, laws and regulations should also be reviewed by internal audit. All policies in regard to the stewardship of assets and the existence of assets should be reviewed by internal audit. Internal audit should also check the efficient management of a company's resources and whether results are consistent with the purpose for which the company was established. Most internal auditors today also report on the risks associated with the business which would have been identified by the board with the assistance of the audit committee or a separate risk committee.

The above clearly points to the importance of the internal audit in the running of a company. A typical internal audit charter is set out in Appendix B (page 134).

# 12

# The Audit Committee

As pointed out in previous chapters, outside directors are at a distinct disadvantage. They suffer from asymmetrical knowledge because the executive directors have the coalface knowledge of the business by dealing with it on a daily basis. The outside director has an intermittent contact with the business through four to six board meetings a year.

In consequence, it is of the utmost importance for the outside director to have assurance of the quality of information which he receives in the board pack.

There are two means of providing this assurance:

one is the audit committee and the other is the internal auditor. The audit committee is a subcommittee of the board and is established to assist the board in discharging its duties relating to stewardship, systems, controls and financial reporting. Some audit committees also deal with the question of risk, but where possible a separate risk committee should be established.

The audit committee should be comprised only of outside directors, all of whom should have not only business knowledge, but experience in financial reporting. The external auditor, the head of internal audit, the chief financial officer and the chief executive officer should attend the audit committee meetings and the chairman of the board should also be invited to attend. The board should appoint the chairman of the audit committee. The committee must be independent so that it can challenge management on the various issues which come before it.

The committee must be dedicated in the sense of commitment to the cause of integrity, understanding the business and having knowledge of the risks involved, as well as the controls. The members need to be financially literate or, at the very least, the majority of them should be. They have to understand financial statements and at least one of the members should be au fait with recent accounting and other reporting standards.

There should be no less than three but no more than five members on the audit committee. Its term of office should be decided in the charter which sets out its remit. Questions of continuity become important when the term of appointment is decided and written into the charter.

The charter must set out clearly the responsibilities of the committee, detailing how and when it should report to the board and what issues it should consider, more particularly the interim and final results.

It must be remembered that the audit committee's role is to recommend the presentation of financial results to the board. It is the board's responsibility to issue the financial statements and to ensure that proper control systems are in place.

The audit committee should ensure that it has adequate resources to discharge its responsibilities and it must be entitled to have access to financial, legal and other professional advice. In this regard it must be entitled to have access to information in the records of the company.

A well functioning internal audit team is essential and the audit committee should work closely with at least the head of the internal audit team. The internal audit should report to the audit committee which should evaluate its abilities.

The audit committee must satisfy itself as to the independence of the external auditor. There must be an atmosphere of creative tension between the audit committee and the external auditor and any differences about reporting as between management and the external auditor must be fully discussed by the audit committee.

The audit committee should meet at least three times a year and its charter should set out the purpose of these meetings. Obviously a detailed agenda must be prepared for each meeting and minutes must be kept.

The chairman of the audit committee should be available at general meetings of the company to answer any questions arising from the financial reporting or any other matter concerning the audit committee.

The minutes of the audit committee should be placed before and noted by the board when next it meets.

An example of a charter of an audit committee and matters which should be considered by an audit committee are set out in Appendices C and D respectively (pages 139 and 151).

# 13

# IT Governance

Willingly or unwillingly, we are members of the information age. The ultimate light in regard to transparency and governance has become information technology. The use of IT in the business world is not only an enabler but has also become of strategic importance. Through this strategic role it has become pervasive.

There are globally recognised auditing and control standards in regard to information systems. Thus one has *certified information systems auditors* and *certified information systems security managers*. Most large companies today have not only chief executives and chief financial officers, but also chief information officers.

The board is responsible for the effective control of its systems. In the nature of things, a board cannot understand everything about a modern information technology system. Consequently, the question of the board discharging its duty of care arises.

When manual processes are changed to systems processes, information technology is introduced into a company and this can be described as the first level of the process. Even at this level intellectual property is locked into the IT and while management and staff are told how to use the system the question arises: Is there really an understanding of the information technology and the systems at board level? In most companies today only the management in the information technology department understands the processes but in consequence a black box scenario is created – and it is the board who is looking into the black box!

The governance issues in regard to information technology become even trickier when the second level is reached; that is, when the systems process and the strategic plans of the company become aligned. The chief information officer (CIO) and his colleagues need to understand the strategic plans of the company, and the board has to understand how the IT strategy is involved in achieving the business plan.

With its pervasive nature it should become clear that IT governance has to be specific to each business. It may be possible to use certain standards as a checklist for level one, but even at this stage it might have to be refined for each specific business.

Board members today have to have a greater understanding of IT than in the past, otherwise they cannot fulfil their duty of care. The current debate is whether the CIO should become a member of the board because while the CIO or outside experts make recommendations on IT capital expenditure, they are not party to the decision to spend the money on what may turn out to be not the best system.

In endeavouring to fulfil its duty of care boards turn to outside service providers and advisers. This in turn leads to huge governance issues. Confidential information goes outside the company, the service providers' values might be different from those of the company which is its client, and the question arises: To whom is the service provider or adviser accountable?

Reliance on outside advisers results in increased financial and reputational risks. Information security becomes a critical issue. Further, a board might have a poor understanding of pricing and the licensing of the service provider, which might force it into renewal agreements.

The development of IT has also led to industry convergence; for example, insurance and banking. This results in directors having to learn a whole new industry.

So whilst IT was initially an enabler, it now supports the very business which is the purpose of the company. It also starts to drive the strategy, and the alignment of the IT strategy and the business strategy becomes critical.

More and more boards are inclining to the view that IT expertise should be vested in a director as a member of the board. In any event boards need to insist that presentations made to them on IT systems should be in very plain language. Further, throughout the world, there is now legislation regulating electronic communication, electronic transactions, electronic filing and the creation of cyber inspectors to inspect, search, seize and investigate unauthorised access.

On the matter of IT governance a board must remember that whilst it can delegate, it cannot abdicate its responsibilities. So a board must ensure that the company has adequate back-up for its system processes; that if a system is innovative and acquired from an entrepreneurial entity that the source code is placed in escrow; that pricing is discussed in detail and on a competitive basis; that the system is not only an enabler but is part of the strategy of the company; the licensing is carefully checked; the reputation of the service provider is known and presentations are made in understandable language.

# 14

## The Corporate Sins

Corporate failures during recent years have resulted from self-interest, self-concern, conformance overriding performance, pride and arrogance.

*Self-interest* is a deadly corporate sin. It occurs when a director fails to exercise his duty of good faith to act in the interests of the incapacitated company he represents and not in his own interests. A director acting in his own interests, and consequently being in conflict with the company, usually does so out of greed to increase his wealth. Such a breach is a fraud on the incapacitated company represented by the director. One of the best examples in modern corporate history of self-interest rather than acting in the best interests of the incapacitated company is the Enron case.

The sin of *self-concern* occurs when directors find themselves in a situation where they are fearful that something adverse may happen to them and the fear drives them to act in conflict with the best interests of the company. For example, directors who are American citizens and subject to the extraterritorial impact of the Foreign Corrupt Practices Act of America, can be conflicted. This Act, simply put, results in American citizens committing criminal conduct when they represent entities offshore which are directly or indirectly involved in corruption. In that situation, being an American citizen and a director of a foreign company, could be a matter of grave concern to a director in making a decision which he believes to be in the best interests of the company, but could result in an investigation into his conduct by the Department of Justice in America and a possible criminal charge against him arising out of innocent indirect involvement.

Too much *conformance* results in a director being merely administrative rather than focusing on the enterprise side of the business. A surfeit of administration dilutes enterprise. With the plethora of legislation about how to govern, the compliance side of governance is starting to weigh down or dilute the enterprise side of a company. This focus on compliance issues and administration tends to make directors and managers slothful. It is estimated that implementing section 404 of the Sarbanes-Oxley Act in America will incur 25 000 hours of work for companies with annual revenues in the 5 to 20 billion dollar range and 100 000 hours of work for companies with annual revenues greater than 20 billion dollars.

The corporate sin of *pride* occurs when, having made a business judgement call that turns out to have been wrong, a board takes too long a time to correct it because of the consequence of finding that it has egg on its face. The quicker the decision is corrected, the better it is for the company. Failure to act because of damaged pride is not acting in the best interests of the incapacitated company.

The corporate sin of *arrogance* is committed when the directors of a company believe they have devised the correct formula on how to conduct the company's business in a particular industry. They believe that they have outwitted their competitors and that almost nothing will go wrong. Well, it always does. How often have we seen this arrogant approach in a particular industry, which usually results in the downfall of the chief executive? Boards must be constantly aware of the corporate sin of arrogance.

Being aware that we all have to deal with human frailty aids the practice of good governance and results in better directors.

# 15

# Corruption Audit

As already pointed out, in the running of any organisation, one is dealing with human beings and consequently with human frailty. A reality which management and leaders have to face is corruption in one form or another taking place in their organisation. Consequently, it has to be managed.

One way to reduce the level of corruption in an organisation is to let it be known that once every six months a corruption audit will be done. Further, it should be a term of every employee's and supplier's contract that the code of conduct of the company is a material term of that contract. In short, any breach of that material term could lead to the termination of the contract. The contract of employment should also include a consent by the employee to be subject to a corruption audit when deemed necessary by the company in its sole discretion.

While each business is different, there are certain issues which a board can have investigated bi-annually in order to get better information on corruption in the organisation. The audit should be carried out by internal audit with oversight by one of the external auditors.

In regard to management the following questions need to be asked: Is there a manager who is dominant? Does any manager override controls or systems? Has any manager's lifestyle changed in the last six months? Is any manager or staff member overzealous, working long hours and weekends and taking no leave? Has any staff member not taken the leave due to him and if not, for what reasons? It often happens that when a corrupt scheme has been created the perpetrator is frightened to go on vacation because in his absence someone else will have to fulfil his task and may discover the corrupt practice. Then the obvious question: Is there a proper segregation of duties?

It is dangerous for the knowledge of a system or a control to be vested in only one person. This breaches the rule that opportunities for corruption should be limited and management needs to take responsibility for changing this practice.

Another issue that needs to be audited is the morale of the people in an organisation. If the morale is low it is more likely that there will be corruption. Investigating this requires a survey of stakeholders such as suppliers, customers and professional advisers; it should not be restricted solely to staff.

The understaffing of a skilled finance department, be it in internal audit or in the actual recording of the financial transactions of an organisation, could lead to corruption. Corruption may also arise if employees are unhappy with their lot, such as their level of pay compared with that of an industry competitor. It is part of the mentality of helping oneself because one feels one is not being adequately compensated.

Another management issue is the necessity to rotate staff in regard to the various tasks in an organisation. Not only does this keep up the interest of staff members, but it is important to move people around in case there is corruption taking place.

Obviously the ethics of the leaders of an organisation are very important.

When employing people for the first time, an in-depth investigation must be made of their references. In this context employees need to place on record their interests, particularly other business interests, whether they are part of management or otherwise. Logically, management and staff should have no objection to the employer having the right in terms of the contract of employment to have access to the employee's and his spouse's bank accounts.

Another issue that should be looked at is whether the grievance procedures in a company are adequate. They must not only be adequate, they must also be fair because if they are not it could lead to dissatisfaction and corruption.

It is important for senior management to ensure that supervision is adequate. Delays in operational issues or in reporting should be carefully checked, more particularly if reconciliations are not done timeously. In this context, inconsistency in production is also something that should raise a red flag.

The question of gambling is a valid one. Corruption is often motivated by an addiction to gambling. Some employers insist that the contract of employment includes the provision that an employee is not entitled to gamble whilst employed by the organisation.

Over-socialising with a stakeholder, particularly a supplier, is another red flag. Here again, some organisations actually make the degree to which an employee may socialise with a supplier or other stakeholder a term of the contract of employment.

Cash transactions between staff members could be a source of corruption. Again, this is sometimes prohibited in employee contracts.

Supervisors and managers must be vigilant for members of staff who have long or hushed telephone conversations.

When members of staff contend that original documents have been lost or when a manager is pressured into signing documents, particularly in batches, suspicion should be raised.

It is a part of the reality of leadership that one is dealing with human beings and consequently with human frailty. The corporate sin of greed is alive in most companies. There is a well-known saying that a man who collects honey will always be tempted to lick his fingers. Corruption is a reality of commercial life and it needs to be managed. Corruption audits should become an essential element of good governance.

# 16

# A Code of Conduct

Stakeholders linked to an entity come from different backgrounds – different homes, cultures, levels of education and value systems. Having regard to these differences, it is a matter of fairness that every person associated with the entity, or entering the portals of the entity, understands what is required from him from the point of view of behaviour.

The conduct of business is in itself an ethical enterprise. An entrepreneur who develops a business concept and implements it in a community creates employment and improves the lives of the people in that community. That is a worthwhile activity, more particularly as it gives the men and women in that local community an opportunity to improve their skills. Society as a whole derives benefits from this activity.

A company should be regarded as a citizen of the country in which it operates. It should therefore act no differently from any natural citizen. Its conduct must be seen to be as decent as that of the natural citizen born in that country.

The ethical standards by which a business is conducted cannot be divorced from the mores of the country in which it operates. It has to reflect the values of the country in which it operates. This is even more important when the country consists of a diverse society.

A code of conduct must not be something which is framed and hung on a wall. It must be a living document and it becomes a living document by incorporating it into stakeholder contracts. For example, the required conduct should be incorporated as a material term in both supplier and employee contracts. A breach of the code of conduct would be regarded as going to the root of the contract, entitling the employer or customer to terminate it.

It is often said that the tone of an organisation should be set at the top. While it is true that if leaders do not act properly, the whole edifice will start to crumble, leaders have a duty to try to inculcate a culture that is commensurate with decency. The culture must be driven through the organisation so that every person in it will know how to do things when no one is watching them.

A corporate culture is developed on the basis of linking the values that drive the business with the business itself. People must be able to live it and feel it. It is the duty of the leaders of an organisation to try to develop that culture, not from the top down, but from the bottom up.

A lot of mergers and acquisitions fail simply because the value systems of the two entities are different. How one behaves in a company and the culture of the company are essential issues for directors.

In developing a code of conduct one has to have regard to a company's internal and external stake-holders. Internally, it will create the standards of behaviour required from the company's internal stakeholders. Consequently, the obligations of managers to owners will be dealt with, such as standards of efficiency, that resources are limited including time resources, avoiding conflicts of interest and respecting confidentiality of sensitive information. Managers must act in good faith, do everything within their power to carry out their duties with skill and care, be accountable to the board and furnish all required information to external and internal auditors.

Similarly, as an internal stakeholder an employee's obligations should be dealt with; for example, supporting management, avoiding unreasonable disruption of production, using his abilities in the interests of the business, acting honestly at all times, not unduly socialising with suppliers or other important stakeholders, and paying due regard to environmental and public health considerations.

The code of conduct must also take account of the external stakeholders. It should do it in such a way that external stakeholders will develop trust and confidence in the company. In this regard the code can deal with customers and the society in which the company operates.

It is best to develop a code on the basis of shared values between the various stakeholders, more particularly the internal stakeholders, and thus a consensus-seeking process is required. In building the code on a consensual basis, not only are values shared but it will have support from the bottom up. In this regard discussions should be held as to the aspirational and directional aspects of the code, the latter being standards that are expected from people and actual conduct which must or must not be carried out.

Implementation of the code of conduct is important. Perhaps the best way to do this is to ensure that people know that it is being applied constantly, is being monitored, and that it is incorporated into contracts of employment and supply.

# 17

# Quantitative Governance

The purpose of this book is to help directors become directors of quality. Outsiders looking into a company will do a quantitative check on the way a company is being governed. Unfortunately the best way to measure the quality of governance is usually with hindsight.

The advantage of doing a quantitative check on processes being employed by a company is that one may find better processes than those currently in use. For this reason, a quantitative check is a useful tool in helping one become a better director and improving one's governance.

A director can use a quantitative checklist to

ascertain whether there are perhaps better processes for the business of his company than the ones currently employed. A useful quantitative checklist is set out below.

1.     Is the company one that is subject to a best practice code, laws or regulations concerning the governance of companies?

2.     Is the board a unitary one or a two-tier board with a supervisory board?

       (Reference to a *board* hereafter applies equally to a unitary and supervisory board unless specifically differentiated.)

3.     *The board*

3.1    Does the company have a unitary board with the correct balance of inside and outside directors to ensure a mix of coalface knowledge and outside practised abilities?

3.2    Does the board have a charter setting out its duties and responsibilities, and does the board clearly understand its duties and responsibilities?

3.3    Does the board understand that it has collective authority but that each director has individual liability and responsibility in regard to decisions made by the board?

3.4    Is the board satisfied that it has full and effective control over the company?

3.5    Does the board monitor management's performance and its implementation of the board's business plans and strategies?

3.6    Has the board devised a succession plan for senior management, more particularly, for the chief executive officer?

3.7    Has the board identified key risk areas relevant to the business of the company?

3.8    Has the board identified key performance indicators relevant to the business of the company?

3.9    Has the board defined levels of materiality beyond which management cannot act without reference to a senior third party or the board itself?

3.10   Has the board reserved specific powers to itself?

3.11   Does the board have adequate reports in regard to the company's compliance with

all laws and regulations relevant to the
business of the company?

3.12    Has the board ensured that, when delegating
any of its authority to a committee or
to management, it has clearly set out in
writing the terms of that authority?

3.13    Is the board satisfied that its size is effective
and that it has the necessary skills and/
or networks represented around the table
in order to make decisions in the best
interests of the company?

3.14    Has the board identified the non-financial
aspects relevant to the business of the
company and does the board regularly
monitor them?

3.15    In deciding that the business will continue
as a going concern in the financial year
ahead, has the board recorded the facts and
assumptions relied on to so report?

3.16    Is the board satisfied that the communication of its decisions is prompt, understandable and substance over form?

3.17    Is the board satisfied that it has balanced
conformance to governance constraints with
performance?

3.18    Is the board satisfied that there is an appro-
        priate balance of power on the board so that
        no one individual or block of individuals
        dominates the board's decision-making pro-
        cess?

3.19    Are the procedures for appointments to the
        board formal and transparent?

3.20    Does the board ensure that at any meeting
        of shareholders a full explanation of the
        effects of any resolution is furnished?

3.21    Does the board encourage attendance of its
        directors and chairmen of its subcommittees
        at general meetings?

3.22    Does the board ensure that there is an
        induction programme for new directors?

3.23    Does the board ensure the integrity of the
        company's risk management and internal
        controls?

3.24    Does the board ensure that there is an
        annual evaluation of its and its directors'
        performance, including the chairman?

3.25    Are the roles of the chairman and chief
        executive separated?

3.26   Does the board in its annual report differentiate between its inside and outside directors and state that there are no shadow directors?

3.27   Does the board satisfy itself that any proposed appointee is not disqualified from being a director?

3.28   Does the board receive regular briefings on new laws and regulations relevant to the business of the company?

3.29   Does the board, at least once every two years, determine the purpose, value drivers and the identity of stakeholders to the company?

3.30   Is the board satisfied that the outside directors possess the reputation, skills, practised abilities and general experience to bring an informed and independent judgement to bear on all issues?

4.     *Board meetings*

4.1    Are at least four board meetings held per year?

4.2    Does the board disclose the number of

meetings held and the attendance of directors at those meetings?

4.3   Does the board ensure that at meetings it reviews the process and procedures in regard to internal systems of control?

4.4   Does the board review the assurances which it receives in regard to the quality of information placed before it?

4.5   Has the board created a process whereby outside directors can have access to management and relevant records of the company?

4.6   Does the board ensure that it receives its board pack timeously?

5.   *Board committees*

5.1   Has the board delegated certain functions to committees, such as the audit comittee?

5.2   Are there written terms of reference which have been approved by the board in regard to each committee?

5.3   Is the board aware that, while it can delegate, it cannot abdicate its responsibilities?

5.4     Are the compositions of the committees disclosed in the annual report?

5.5     Are the board committees regularly evaluated as to their performance and effectiveness?

5.6     Are all board committees chaired by independent outside directors?

5.7     Are the board committees free to take independent outside professional advice on matters relevant to their remits?

5.8     Are dealings in the company's securities prohibited for directors, officers and other selected employees for a designated period prior to the announcement of financial results or for any other period considered sensitive, such as a closed period?

5.9     Is the prohibition on dealings in the company's securities recorded in writing and implemented by the company secretary?


6.      *Remuneration*

6.1     Is the remuneration paid to senior management of such a nature that it is not only motivational but should retain their services?

6.2     Does the company have a remuneration committee made up of independent outside directors?

6.3     Does the remuneration committee have written terms of reference which have been approved by the board?

6.4     Does the board ensure that it approves all recommendations of the remuneration committee?

6.5     Does the chairman of the remuneration committee attend general meetings?

6.6     Does the annual report contain details of every director's remuneration and benefits on an individual basis?

6.7     Is performance-linked remuneration a substantial part of senior management's remuneration?

6.8     Does the remuneration to outside directors depend on their relevant contribution to the business of the board and the company and/or its committees?

6.9     Is there full disclosure of inside directors' service contracts?

7.      *Company secretary*

7.1     Does the company secretary play a role
        in ensuring good governance in the
        company?

7.2     Does the company secretary support the
        chairman in ensuring the effective func-
        tioning of the board?

7.3     Does the company secretary provide the
        board and its directors with guidance on
        the discharge of their responsibilities?

7.4     Does the company secretary play a role in
        the induction of new directors?

7.5     Does the company secretary provide a
        source of guidance and advice to the board
        on matters of governance?

7.6     Has the board ensured that the company
        secretary would pass a fit and proper test?

8.      *Risk management*

8.1     Does the board take responsibility for the
        risk management process and its effect-
        iveness?

8.2 Does the board ensure that management integrates the risk management processes into the business of the company?

8.3 Does the board design the risk policies in conjunction with senior management?

8.4 Are the risk policies communicated to all employees and incorporated into the culture of the company?

8.5 Does the board consider not only the negative aspects of risk, but also the positive aspect in the sense of its appetite to take risks for concomitant reward?

8.6 Does the board make use of generally recognised risk management and internal control frameworks in order to provide reasonable assurance regarding the achievement of:
- effectiveness and efficiency of operations?
- safeguarding the company's assets, including information?
- compliance with applicable laws, regulations and supervisory requirements?
- business sustainability?
- reliability of reporting? and
- behaving responsibly towards and responsively to the identified stakeholders

in regard to their legitimate reasonable expectations?

8.7     Does the board ensure that a formal risk assessment is undertaken annually to support its public statement on risk management?

8.8     Has the board appointed either a specific committee or one of its committees to assist in reviewing the risk management process and the significant risks facing the company?

8.9     Are the processes of risk management and the systems of internal control communicated throughout the company?

8.10     Is there an adequate system of internal controls in place?

8.11     Has the company identified its major risks particularly those that can have a disastrous impact on its business activities?

8.12     Is the board satisfied with its disclosure in its annual report in regard to risk management?

8.13     Does the risk assessment cover operating risks, people risks, technology and management information systems risks, disaster recovery, back-up, compliance risks, strategic risks and credit risks?

8.14    Does the company have a system for the confidential reporting of any corrupt act in the business of the company?

9.    *Internal audit*

9.1    Does the company have an effective internal audit function?

9.2    Does this function have the respect and cooperation of the board and management?

9.3    If the company does not have an internal audit function, does the board explain in its annual report how it obtains assurances regarding effective internal processes and systems?

9.4    Are the purpose and mandate of the internal auditing activity defined in a written charter and are they consistent with the Institute of Internal Auditors' (IIA) definition of internal auditing?

9.5    Does internal audit report at a level in the company that allows it to accomplish its responsibilities?

9.6     Does the head of internal audit have ready
        and regular access to the chairman of the
        company and the chairman of the audit
        committee?

9.7     Does the head of internal audit attend
        audit committee meetings?

9.8     Is the company's internal audit plan based
        on continuous risk assessment?

9.9     Does the board ensure that the internal
        audit plan dovetails with the external audit
        plan and that there is no duplication of
        effort?

9.10    Does the internal audit actually function
        in accordance with the IIA's definition of
        internal audit?

9.11    Does the audit committee approve the in-
        ternal audit work plan and recommend it
        to the board?

9.12    Does the board ensure that the internal
        audit and external audit plans adequately
        cover financial, operational and compliance
        issues?

9.13    Does the board ensure that the head of in-
        ternal audit is appointed and/or dismissed

only after recommendation by the audit committee and approval by the board?

10.   *Sustainability reporting*

10.1   Does the board report at least annually on the adherence to its code of conduct, on its corporate social investment and its compliance with safety, health and environmental legislation?

10.2   Does the board at least annually address the question of the non-financial aspects relevant to the business of the company?

10.3   Does the board have its non-financial aspects verified by an independent third party?

10.4   If so, is this verification disclosed in its annual report?

10.5   Has the board established criteria for measuring human capital development and does it report in this regard, for example, the success of employee training, the financial investment in employees, the average age of various grades of employees, etc.

10.6   Does the board ensure that relevant stakeholders have been a party to the development of the company's code of conduct?

10.7 Does the company demonstrate its commitment to its code of conduct through a structured process of enforcement?

10.8 Does the company disclose the extent of the compliance with its code of conduct?

10.9 Does the company take appropriate action when dealing with individuals who contravene the code of conduct?

10.10 Does the board apply its mind to the company continuing to trade or deal with individuals or companies who do not meet the standards set out in its code of conduct?

10.11 Has the board developed a corporate social responsibility plan and does it monitor corporate social investment?

11. *Accounting and auditing*

11.1 Do the external auditors observe the highest level of business and professional ethics and independence?

11.2 Does the board require the external auditor

to disclose its code of conduct?

11.3   Does the board ensure consultation be-
       tween and an integration of the services of
       internal and external audit?

11.4   Has the audit committee established clear
       guidelines for the use by the company
       of non-audit services carried out by the
       external auditor?

11.5   Is there a separate disclosure in the annual
       report of the fees and the nature of the non-
       audit services carried out by the external
       auditors?

11.6   Does the audit committee have written
       terms of reference?

11.7   Does the board ensure that the audit com-
       mittee has financial literacy?

11.8   Does the audit committee determine
       whether any interim report should be
       subject to an independent review by the
       external auditors?

11.9   Does the board monitor the audit com-
       mittee's performance and evaluate it at
       least on an annual basis?

11.10   Is the chairman of the audit committee available at general meetings to answer questions about its work?

12.   *Relationships with shareholders*

12.1   Does the company have dialogue with its major institutional shareholders?

12.2   Is the board satisfied that its shareholders can evaluate the governance of the company from the contents of the annual report?

12.3   Is the board satisfied that any resolution is accompanied by an explanation of its effect?

12.4   Does the company conduct general meetings on the basis of a poll?

13.   *Communication*

13.1   Does the company base its reporting on the principles of transparency and substance over form?

13.2   Does the company's annual report cover matters which illustrate that the company is acting responsibly towards and responsively to its stakeholders?

13.3 Does the annual report identify the legitimate reasonable expectations of its stakeholders?

13.4 Does the board monitor how these expectations are being managed and whether these expectations are being met?

13.5 Do the directors, in the annual report, acknowledge their responsibility to prepare the financial statements, that the statements fairly present the state of affairs of the business at the end of the financial year and that it is the external auditors who have to report on whether the financial statements amount to fair presentation?

13.6 Does the annual report present an objective statement of the company's activities during the year?

13.7 Does the annual report record that the company has complied with applicable accounting standards and what they are?

13.8 Does the board report and acknowledge that adequate accounting records, effective systems of internal control and risk management have been maintained, that the appropriate accounting policies have been adopted and that any judgements or estimates have been implemented consistently?

# 18

# Self-evaluation

None of us is perfect or prescient. In consequence we all make mistakes in the business judgement calls we make.

When making that wrong business judgement call it is, however, important to be able to say, hand on heart, that one applied good governance in the sense of honestly applying one's mind in the best interests of the company.

That is why it is so important to evaluate one's performance as a director. It helps one to become a better director if one's performance is evaluated at least once a year.

Each director should do a self-evaluation, the chairman included. There are several precedents for self-evaluation. It is, however, essentially a candid discussion about one's performance during the year that really helps one to improve as a director and heightens one's awareness of the need to practise good governance.

The board should review how it monitors management's performance and how management is implementing the board's strategic plan. Has the board identified the information it needs and the information to benchmark management's performance? Has the board set reasonable objectives and are they being monitored?

Questions should be asked as to whether the size of the board and its composition is adequate for the company. Are the outside directors independent enough? Have new directors been properly inducted and has there been any director training during the year – for example, on new International Financial Reporting Standards?

Have there been constructive debates on issues and is management absolutely transparent with the board? Is there a good working relationship between the board and the chief executive?

Are there free and open discussions on issues at board meetings? Is there any dominance by any one director? Is dissent ever seen as disloyalty? Is there creative tension in the boardroom?

Does the chairman control the meeting? Does he ensure that meetings finish within a reasonable time?

Have the board committees been of assistance and are they adequately skilled? Is the board timeously informed of matters by its committees? Does the information received from the committees fulfil the needs of the board?

Does the board evaluate management's performance and their compensation? Does the board have regular reports on compliance with the company's code of conduct and on corruption audits?

Does the board identify the company's purpose, its value drivers and stakeholders at least once every two years?

Has the board identified the risks involved in the business and ranked the three most important?

Has the board discussed succession and does it have a plan in place?

Has the board identified the non-financial aspects relevant to the business of the company? Has the board developed a corporate social investment programme which is aligned to the company's business?

Does the board challenge management when necessary, and does it provide counsel where necessary?

Is there the proper mix of skills for the business of the company around the boardroom table?

The above are examples of questions that a board should ask itself. There are many examples of self-evaluation questionnaires, but boards may find it more helpful to have a facilitator to interview each board member separately and then report the overall results to the board.

# 19

# Today's International Company

In the twenty-first century some international companies operate in many different countries. There is no global governance framework for a holding company with many foreign subsidiaries, which leads to a number of issues, such as operating under different legal and governance frameworks.

It is generally accepted that a global holding company of today cannot operate on a command and control basis. The rules laid down by the holding company might even be illegal in one or more of the countries in which a subsidiary operates. Further, health, social and environmental legislation differs from country to country. Reporting standards from an accounting point of view could be different, and so could governance codes or laws.

It is no answer to substitute a command and control process from a head office to state entities enforced by criminal sanction or otherwise. A command and control structure does not create good governance in the holding company or its subsidiaries.

What the global holding company of today has to do is to create a global framework for its subsidiaries and it can only achieve this by laying down governance principles. The holding company should also create the value drivers which it wants its subsidiaries to adopt. In short, it must lay down principles which will clearly spell out to the boards of its subsidiaries how they should do things in their country when the holding company is not around or watching them.

The holding company has to describe the purpose of the business and this can no longer be defined only in outcome or financial terms such as return on capital employed. It needs to identify its value drivers and the major stakeholders relevant to its business and prescribe the principle that it and its subsidiaries must act responsibly towards and responsively to the stakeholders.

The holding company needs to define what are the

legitimate reasonable expectations of stakeholders. In the nature of things, each subsidiary operating in a different country would have a myriad of expectations from its stakeholders. The holding company should identify the stakeholders who would be relevant throughout the world, but each subsidiary would have to identify the stakeholders relevant to the business in its particular country and then work out the legitimate reasonable expectations of those stakeholders. It is these expectations which must be taken into account in the direction of the company in each jurisdiction.

Business people today speak about an implied contract between the company and its stakeholders. Stakeholders either have a contractual link to the company, such as a supplier, or they are linked by the common law through delict or tort. They are also linked through legislation such as health legislation. All this results in a myriad of expectations but no company can be expected to deal with these diverse expectations, some of which are not even legitimate. The company has to take a hard-nosed approach to identifying the legitimate reasonable expectations of stakeholders relevant to its business and then manage the relationship with them.

When a company has a downturn, and each company does, it will be able to revive more quickly with the support of its stakeholders. A board has to remember that quality and price have today become so highly competitive that other differentiating factors have to be found. There is an expectation by modern local communities that companies as employers need to deal with issues other than purely business ones and need to take a leadership role. Ford, for example, has adopted family values as its differentiating factor. Companies today have to engage with stakeholders. This does not mean that boards are accountable to stakeholders, because they are accountable only to the company – but boards have to be seen to be acting responsibly towards and responsively to the company's stakeholders.

The holding company should require each subsidiary board to understand and practise the concepts of intellectual honesty and intellectual naivety. Each board must identify with the group's purpose, its value drivers and the identification of its major stakeholders. The board of each subsidiary would be expected to accept that they were representing an incapacitated entity and should act accordingly in exercising their duties of good faith, care, skill and diligence. They should all ask the ten silent questions and, if necessary, the chairman should verbalise the questions. They have to ensure that the subsidiary acts as a decent citizen in the context of the mores and values of the particular country in which it operates.

Global companies can no longer be monocultural in a global business world. To be sustainable they have to attract skills and talents from different cultures. Further, global companies have to understand the limits of the legitimacy of their businesses and address this question. Currently, there is a crisis of trust and confidence in companies. The global company should identify some corporate social investment which can be mutually beneficial to its business to improve legitimacy. For example, a construction company operating in different countries could adopt brick-making projects in poorer countries, buy the bricks they produce, improve the quality of life of those employed on the projects, and thereby improve the legitimacy of the construction business.

The holding company has to impress on each subsidiary that it must be seen to be a decent citizen in the social and cultural milieu in which it operates in a particular country. This becomes critical in the protection of the group's brand. The holding company needs to impress on the subsidiaries that the directors must act correctly not because they are decent but they are decent because they act correctly.

Today global companies have to ensure that they and their subsidiaries have, as it were, a human face. The board must always remember that the ultimate social responsibility is sustainable performance.

This can, however, only be achieved in the twenty-first century by promoting the legitimacy of the business, making the company that owns the business a decent citizen, differentiating it, and performing on the bottom line.

Global companies should lay down principles as suggested above and each subsidiary must then run the business in its own country. Obviously the holding company will have checks and balances from a financial viewpoint, but it will not be able to lay down rules which would be appropriate in more than a hundred different countries.

The great global company of tomorrow is the one that is going to get the balance of conformance and performance for its business just right and be able to define its purpose and carry on its business not only in economic terms. This will create a trust and confidence in the company and its brand on a global basis.

To try and create a global legislative framework for companies has not only huge international legal problems of legislation but also enforcement, and one cannot create substance by laying down form. Legislation such as Sarbanes-Oxley will not stop dishonesty by endeavouring to create substance with form. Further, rigidity in process dilutes enterprise.

In summary, the key challenge facing the global company today is to ensure that quality governance principles are applied by the local boards of its many subsidiaries. These principles are those of *fairness*, *accountability*, *responsibility* and *transparency*, based on a foundation of *intellectual honesty*.

- Fairness includes decisions that will ensure that the company is seen as a decent citizen and its business accepted as legitimate;

- accountability means being accountable to the company which one represents;

- responsibility connotes acting in a responsible manner and being seen to be acting responsibly towards and responsively to its identified stakeholders;

- transparency connotes substance over form coupled with the truthful and prompt communication of important decisions; and

- intellectual honesty is employing one's practised abilities and honestly applying one's mind in the decision-making process in the best interests of the incapacitated company which one represents.

The global company in the twenty-first century has to build a culture with these principles deeply embedded throughout the group. If it does not, the debate will start as to whether a company is the correct entity through which business should be conducted, as the debate has now started as to whether the nation state is the correct entity in which we should live.

# 20

# Good Governance

There are several benefits in practising good governance. Even when one makes the wrong business judgement call on the enterprise side of the company, if good governance has been practised a scandal can be avoided. People accept that others make mistakes and will accept that directors will make mistakes in business judgement calls. A director is, however, expected to honestly apply his mind in the best interests of the company of which he is a director.

When there is a downturn in the life of the company, provided one has practised good governance, one is able to correct it and turn it around more quickly with support from stakeholders. In this context, too, good governance results in a more sustainable enterprise for the company. Practise good governance and your licensors will support you in need.

One of the great attributes of practising good governance is that a well-governed company usually is able to attract better employees than one that is not. It has also been established that company A, which practises good corporate governance compared with company B in the same industry which does not, will be able to raise capital more cheaply. For this reason alone the director needs to ensure that his company is being well governed.

One of the most important assets of any company is its reputation. The best way to protect a company's reputation is not only to ensure the quality of the product or service provided, but also that quality governance is practised. When a mistake is made on the enterprise side of the company, good governance will usually take the company through the crisis and help the directors to regroup and carry on. Bad governance and a bad business judgement call is usually a death knell for a company.

Having regard to the importance of good governance, let us summarise the essential elements.

The practice of good governance can be achieved by being aware of the four fundamental duties of a director; namely, good faith, care, skill and diligence. The guidelines in a code are there to help one carry out and be seen to be carrying out these duties. These guidelines must not be weapons of mass distraction from the purpose of the company. A director's ultimate responsibility is to ensure the business success of the company which he is leading. A board needs to get the right balance for the company's business, between conformance (constraints of process) and performance (enterprise).

A director must be aware of the corporate sins which are present in any company. A good board identifies the licensors of the business and is aware of the framework of governance in which the company operates. The director needs to ask the suggested ten silent questions at every board meeting. At times these questions should be verbalised so that fellow directors are aware of an important factor in the decision-making process. They may be subconsciously aware, but it helps to consciously bring it to everyone's attention.

A director must be alive to his own frailty, past prejudices and present needs and the frailty of his fellow directors. Not only must this be accommodated, but it must also be managed.

The intellectual energy which is brought about by a group of directors in a board meeting to discuss an issue and make a decision must be used honestly in the best interests of the company. It is this intellectual honesty that should form the basis of governing any company. Intellectual honesty is immutable in the decision-making process. In this context it helps to remember that in leading a company one is acting for an incapacitated juristic person and one needs to carry out the duties of good faith, care, skill and diligence in the interests of the company as if it were an incapacitated human being.

The board must define the purpose of the business, which can no longer be done simply in economic terms. Account has to be taken of the legitimacy of the business. The value drivers of the business must be defined and its stakeholders identified. The strategic business plan should be developed taking account of these three aspects – purpose, value drivers and stakeholders.

The conducting of business is in itself an ethical enterprise. Nothing can be more ethical than creating employment for people in a local community in which a business operates and which gives men and women in that community the opportunity to improve their lives. Consequently, it behoves all directors of companies to conduct and direct their companies ethically in order to govern on a quality basis. The ethical conduct of the enterprise and practising good governance have always formed the foundation of the great sustained companies of the world. One only has to look at the great schools, universities, charitable organisations, clubs and companies in one's own country to see that this applies to all entities that are directed by human beings.

The board must use its best endeavours to ensure that it receives quality information. In this regard competent internal audit processes and a competent, financially literate and diligent audit committee are essential for good governance to be practised.

The practice of good governance is a journey. It is not a destination because a director is dealing with uncertain future events, and in carrying out his duties he has to make decisions from a foundation of intellectual honesty within the pillars of fairness, accountability, responsibility and transparency. A quantitative compliance approach to governance will not create intellectual honesty. Substance cannot be created by form, and since performance is the ultimate responsibility, processes should not be cast in stone. What must be cast in stone, however, is intellectual honesty.

The concepts of intellectual honesty, intellectual naivety, the inclusive approach, incapacity, assurances on quality of information (internal audit, external audit and the audit committee), the corporate sins, the decent citizen and the silent questions are set out in a graphic in Appendix E (page 173), as an aid to the practice of good governance.

# APPENDICES

# Appendix A

# The Framework of Corporate Governance

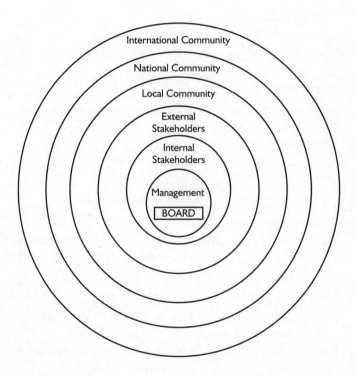

# Appendix B

# Internal Audit Charter

## 1. *Mission and scope of work*

The mission of the internal auditors is to provide independent, objective assurance on information, controls, systems and processes. They must determine whether the network of risk management, controls, systems and processes is adequate and functioning in a manner to ensure that:

1.1     risks are appropriately identified and managed;

1.2     significant financial, managerial and operating information is accurate, reliable and timely;

1.3     employees' actions are in compliance with policies, standards, procedures and applicable laws and regulations;

1.4     resources are acquired economically, used efficiently, and adequately protected;

1.5     progammes, plans and objectives are achieved;

1.6     quality and continuous improvement are

fostered in the company's control process; and

1.7    significant legislative or regulatory issues impacting the company are recognised and addressed appropriately.

Opportunities for improving controls, systems and processes may be identified during audits. These should be communicated to the appropriate level of management.

## 2.    *Accountability*

The head of internal audit, in the discharge of his/ her duties, shall be accountable to management and the audit committee to:

2.1    provide annually an assessment of the adequacy and effectiveness of the company's processes for controlling its activities and managing its risks;

2.2    report significant issues related to the processes for controlling the activities of the company and its affiliates, including potential improvements to those processes;

2.3    periodically provide information on the annual audit plan and the sufficiency of the resources of internal audit;

2.4    coordinate with other control and monitoring functions (risk management, compliance, security, legal, ethics, environmental, external audit).

3.      *Independence*

To provide for the independence of the internal auditors, they should report to the head of internal audit who should report functionally and administratively to the chief executive officer and periodically to the audit committee.

4.      *Responsibility*

The internal auditors have the responsibility to:

4.1     develop an internal annual audit plan using an appropriate risk-based methodology, including any risks or control concerns identified by management, and submit that plan to the audit committee for review and approval as well as periodic updates;

4.2     develop the plan so that it complements the external audit plan;

4.3     implement the audit plan as approved, including as appropriate any special tasks or projects requested by management and the audit committee;

4.4     evaluate and assess significant new or

changing services, processes, operations and control processes;

4.5     issue periodic reports to the audit committee and management summarising results of internal audit activities;

4.6     keep the audit committee informed of emerging trends and successful practices in internal auditing;

4.7     assist in the investigation of significant suspected wrongful activities and report thereon.

## 5.     *Authority*

The internal auditors are authorised to:

5.1     have unrestricted access to all functions, records, assets and personnel;

5.2     have full and free access to the audit committee;

5.3     obtain the necessary assistance of personnel in the performance of their audit.

The internal auditors are not authorised to:

- perform any operational duties;
- initiate or approve accounting transactions; and
- direct the activities of any company employee not employed in internal audit,

except to the extent that such employees
have been appropriately assigned to assist
them.

6.    *Standards of audit practice*

The internal auditors should meet or exceed the
Standard for the Professional Practice of Internal
Auditing of the Institute of Internal Auditors.

# Appendix C

# Audit Committee Charter

1.  *Constitution*

The Audit Committee ('Committee') should assist
the board in discharging its duties relating to the
safeguarding of assets, the operating of adequate
systems, control processes and the preparation of
financial reports and statements in compliance
with all applicable legal requirements and accounting standards. The Committee should not perform any management functions or assume any
management responsibilities. The Committee should
make recommendations to the board for its approval or decision. The membership, resources,
responsibilities and authority of the Committee
are set out hereunder.

2.  *Membership*

- The members shall consist of three non-
  executive directors appointed by the
  board, with at least the majority being
  independent non-executive directors.

- The board shall appoint a chairman from the members of the Committee and determine the period for which he or she shall hold office. The chairman of the board should not be appointed as chairman of the Committee.
- The board has the power at any time to remove any member from the Committee and to fill any vacancy created by such removal.
- The company secretary shall be the secretary of the Committee.

3.    The Committee should:

3.1    evaluate the independence and effectiveness of the external auditor and consider any non-audit services rendered by such auditor as to whether this impairs their independence;

3.2    evaluate the performance of the external auditor;

3.3    consider and make recommendations on the appointment, retention, resignation or removal of the external auditor;

3.4    discuss and revise, with the external auditor, before the audit commences, the auditor's engagement letter, the terms, nature and scope of the audit function and the audit fee;

3.5    agree to the timing and nature of reports from the external auditor;

3.6    consider any issues identified in the going concern or the adequacy of internal control statements;

3.7    consider any accounting treatments, significant unusual transactions, or accounting judgments, that could be contentious;

3.8    identify key matters arising in the current year's management letter;

3.9    consider whether any significant ventures, investments or operations are not subject to external audit;

3.10    discuss the implications of new auditing standards and ensure that the external audit fee will sustain a proper audit; and

3.11    obtain assurance from the external auditor that adequate accounting records are being maintained.

4.    The Committee should examine and review the annual financial statements, the

interim reports, the accompanying reports to shareholders, the preliminary announcement of results and any other announcement regarding the company's financial information to be made public, prior to submission and approval by the board, focusing particularly on:

- the implementation of new systems;
- tax and litigation matters involving uncertainty;
- any changes in accounting policies and practices;
- major judgmental areas;
- significant adjustments resulting from the audit;
- the basis on which the company has been determined a going concern;
- capital adequacy;
- internal controls;
- compliance with the required accounting standards;
- the efficiency of major adjustments processed at year end;
- compliance with loan covenants; and
- reviewing documents containing financial information.

5.    The Committee should monitor and supervise the effective function of the internal audit, ensuring that the roles and functions

of the external audit with internal audit
are sufficiently clarified and coordinated
to provide an objective overview of the
operational effectiveness of the company's
systems of internal control and reporting.

This will include:

- reviewing the effectiveness of the company's systems of internal control, including internal financial control and
  business risk management;
- considering the appointments, dismissal
  or reassignment of the head of the internal audit function;
- reviewing and approving the internal
  audit plan and internal audit's conclusions with regard to internal control;
- reviewing the adequacy of corrective
  action taken in response to significant
  internal audit findings;
- reviewing significant matters reported
  by the internal audit function;
- reviewing the objectives and the operations of the internal audit function;
- assessing the adequacy of available
  internal audit resources;
- reviewing the cooperation and coordination between the internal and external
  audit functions and coordinating the
  internal audit plan with the external

auditors to avoid duplication of work;

- reviewing significant differences of opinion between management and the internal audit function;
- evaluating the independence, effectiveness and performance of the internal auditors;
- directing and supervising investigations into matters within the scope of internal audit.

6.1 The chairman of the Committee shall account to the board for its activities and make recommendations to the board concerning the adoption of the annual and interim financial statements and any other matters arising from the above responsibilities.

6.2 The chairman (or, in his/her absence, an alternate member) of the Committee shall attend the annual general meeting to answer questions concerning matters falling within the ambit of the Committee.

7. In discharging its responsibilities, the Committee will:

7.1 *Financial statements*

- review the quality of financial information, interim and financial statements and other public and regulatory reporting;

- review the annual report and accounts taken as a whole, to ensure they present a balanced and understandable assessment of the position, performance and prospects of the company;
- review the external auditor's proposed audit certificate;
- discuss problems and reservations arising from the audit, and any matters the auditor may wish to discuss (in the absence, where requested by the Committee, of executive directors and any other person who is not a member of the committee);
- review the external auditor's management letter and management response; and,
- review the credibility, independence and objectivity of the auditor, taking into account their audit and non-audit fees; keep the nature and extent of such non-audit services under review.

7.2    *Internal control and internal audit*

- review the company's statement on internal control systems prior to endorsement by the board, and in particular to review:

(i)   the procedures for identifying business risks and controlling their impact on the company;

(ii)  the company's policies for preventing or detecting fraud;

(iii) the company's policies for ensuring that it complies with relevant regulatory and legal requirements;

(iv)  the operational effectiveness of the policies and procedures;

- review the results of work performed by the internal audit function in relation to financial reporting, corporate governance, internal control, and any significant investigations and management responses;

- review coordination between the internal audit function and the external auditors and deal with any issues of material or significant dispute or concern;

- review any significant transactions not directly related to the company's normal business;

- review significant cases of employee conflicts of interest, misconduct or fraud, or any other unethical activity by employees;

- review the controls over significant risks; and

- consider other relevant matters referred to it by the Board.

8.1 Meetings of the Committee will be held as frequently as the Committee considers appropriate, but it will normally meet not less than three times a year. The board or any member thereof, including members of the Committee, the external auditor, and the head of internal audit may call further meetings.

8.2 Reasonable notice of meetings and the business to be conducted shall be given to the members of the Committee and invitees such as the chief financial officer, the head of internal audit and the external auditor.

8.3 The quorum for decisions of the Committee shall be any two members of the Committee present throughout the meeting of the Committee.

8.4 The finance director, senior audit partner in charge of the external audit and head of internal audit shall be in attendance at meetings of the Committee and shall have unrestricted access to the chairman or any other member of the Committee in relation to any matter falling within the remit of the Committee.

8.5 The chairman, at his/her discretion, may invite other executives to attend and to be heard at meetings of the Committee.

8.6     No invitee shall have a vote at meetings of the Committee.

8.7     The minutes of all meetings of the Committee, or summaries thereof, shall be submitted to the board at the immediate following board meeting, the agenda for each such board meeting shall provide an opportunity for the chairman of the Committee to report on any matter within the Committee's remit.

9.1     Meetings and proceedings of the Committee should be governed by the company's articles of association regulating the meetings and proceedings of directors and committees.

9.2     The company secretary should take minutes of meetings. These should be reviewed and approved by the members of the Committee.

10.     The Committee, in carrying out its tasks:

10.1    is authorised to investigate any activity within its terms of reference;

10.2    may require other employees of the company to attend meetings or parts of meetings;

10.3    may consult with and seek any information it requires from any employee, and all employees shall be required to cooperate with any request made by the Committee in the course of its duties;

10.4    shall at least once a year meet with the external auditor without any executives in attendance; and

10.5    shall at least once a year meet with the internal auditors without any executives in attendance.

11.1    Members of the Committee shall be paid such remuneration in respect of their appointment as shall be determined by the board.

11.2    The chairman of the Committee shall, in addition to his or her remuneration as a member, receive a further sum as determined by the board.

11.3    Such remuneration in terms hereof shall be in addition to the annual fees payable to directors.

12.1 The Committee, in carrying out its tasks may obtain such outside or professional advice as it considers necessary to carry out its duties.

12.2 The board shall ensure that the Committee has access to professional advice both inside and outside the company in order for it to perform its duties.

# Appendix D

# Matters for Consideration by an Audit Committee

1.1    The audit committee has three distinct providers of assurance over the accuracy, reliability and completeness of the financial statements at its disposal, namely management, internal and external audit. The audit committee has to have the necessary ability and financial literacy to use effectively these three forms of assurance in making an assessment of whether or no to recommend the financial statements to the board of directors for approval.

1.2    The audit committee has a significant responsibility in assessing the fair presentation of financial statements. It needs to ask pertinent, meaningful and specific questions of these assurance providers and to consider the impact of their responses on the financial statements.

1.3    In order to ensure that this is done it needs to adopt a framework covering the following seven broad categories:

- Review of financial reporting.
- Management overview of the financial results of an entity for the period.
- The suitability and applicability of accounting policies.
- The business transactions and accounting estimates presented in financial statements.
- Current developments in auditing, accounting, reporting and taxation.
- External auditor's communication.
- Compliance with current regulatory environment.

1.4     The audit committee should obtain an undertaking from senior management, including executive directors and invitees present at audit committee meetings, that they are not aware of any issues, happenings or transactions that could affect or influence the audit committee in recommending to the board the approval of the financial results. This should be in the form of a formal management representation letter.

2.     *Review of financial reporting*

2.1     The audit committee assumes the responsibility to review the financial reporting of the company and consequently should review the following information:

- Published financial results, including interim results;
- Public financial circulars e.g., those pertaining to acquisitions;
- Earnings releases and financial announcements;
- Regulatory requirements pertaining to specific industries;
- Any other applicable ad hoc issues as decided by the audit committee or as requested by the board.

2.2    The audit committee needs to understand the industry in which the company operates. This will allow it to better understand the company's financial results and the representations made by management through the financial statements.

2.3    The committee needs to understand how changes within the company (such as mergers and acquisitions) and changes in its industry have been reflected in the financial statements.

2.4    The committee needs to exercise its judgement according to the complexity of the industry in which the company operates and to this end should:

- Seek input concerning the risk universe in which the company operates;
- Seek expert or specialist input and guidance on the company's compliance with its regulatory environment.

3. *Management overview of the financial results of an entity for the period*

3.1 The audit committee should discuss the results with senior management in the context of the performance of competitors, the company's business plan and its budget. This will equip the committee to engage with management on the results as presented by management.

3.2 Audit committee members should consider whether the results:

- are consistent with their expectations having regard to the circumstances of the company and the current environment of the industry within which it operates;
- are consistent with or adequately reconciled with the previous representations and forecasts made by management;
- are in line with its discussions with the other assurance providers, namely the internal and external auditors.

4.  *The suitability and applicability of*
    *accounting policies*

4.1  *Background*

The audit committee members need to
assess whether the accounting policies employed by management are appropriate and
applicable. In order for them to be able to
exercise this responsibility they need to
be financially literate. Financial literacy is
broadly defined as the ability to read and
understand financial statements, including
a balance sheet, income statement and cash
flow statement. The members also need to
have a good financial understanding of
the industry and the economy in which
the company operates. At least one of the
attendees needs to be proficient in understanding the implications of current and
planned accounting and auditing standards.

4.2  *Considerations*

- Are we as an audit committee financially
  literate and in a position to understand
  the accounting policies employed by
  management?
- Is at least one of the members technically
  proficient and able to assess the entity's
  compliance with latest standards? Tech-

nical expertise should be sought if necessary.

- Are the accounting policies employed by management appropriate in terms of generally accepted accounting practice? Accounting policies are updated and amended on a continuous basis and management need to ensure that they respond timeously to these changes.
- Do we understand all changes to accounting policies, the rationale behind management changing the accounting policies and whether they have been appropriately disclosed?

Management may have proposed to change an accounting policy during a period or adopt a new accounting policy. The audit committee needs to understand and critically assess the rationale for the change and approve management's decision.

- How do the accounting policies employed by the company compare with industry and benchmark treatments proposed by the accounting standards?

## 5.1    *Business transactions*

### 5.1.1    *Management considerations*

- Has management responded appropriately to underlying business transactions?

The committee needs to understand how management has responded to the transactions and whether they have put sufficient control measures in place to address them.

- What is management's assessment of the overall control environment?

The audit committee should obtain management's assessment of the internal control environment in order to gauge the reliance which can be placed on the system of control.

### 5.1.2   *Internal audit considerations*

The committee needs to consider the following when assessing and approving the financial statements.

- Has the scope and extent of the risk-based internal audit been performed in terms of the approved internal audit plan?
- Is the audit committee still happy with the approved internal audit plan and its impact on the risk assurance it is seeking?

Are there any significant changes in the entity's risk profile, which would result in a change to the internal audit plan?

- What were the internal audit findings and conclusions and are there any pending issues?

The audit committee should obtain an understanding of the results of audit tests conducted on the different areas. It should also have an understanding of management's response to internal audits and the potential impact on the financial statements of any poorly controlled areas.

The audit committee should also review all pending internal audit issues reported that have not been resolved by management and assess management's response which should be in writing.

- What is internal audit's assessment of the overall control environment? The committee should obtain internal audit's assessment of the internal control environment in order to gauge the reliance that can be placed on the system of control.
- What is internal audit's assessment of the potential impact of the areas of significance or relevance that have not been tested during the period?

### 5.1.3 *External audit considerations*

The committee needs to seek assurance from its external assurance providers over transactions reflected in the financial statements. The following items need to be considered by the committee.

- Were the material areas not tested by the internal audit department audited by the external auditors?
- The audit committee needs to know that the external auditors gathered sufficient and appropriate audit evidence to support their opinion. The audit committee needs to have an understanding of the results of these audit tests and any pending concerns.
- How comfortable are the external auditors with the internal control environment and the extent of reliance placed thereon?
- How comfortable are the external auditors that the financial statements fairly present the results of transactions?

### 5.2 *Accounting estimates*

An accounting estimate is an approximation of the amount of an item/items in the absence of a precise means of measurement.

5.2.1    Accounting estimates are raised and
         processed by management based on their
         interpretation of a series of indicators. These
         estimates pose significant risk for the audit
         committee as they are outside the scope of
         transactions and processes and typically
         no systems control environment is in place
         to manage them, except for high-level
         managerial review. The audit committee
         needs to understand these estimates, their
         effect on the financial statements and,
         where it is applicable, to ensure that there
         are appropriate disclosures.

5.2.2    *Management*

         • What are the significant accounting
           estimates included in the financial
           statements?

         The audit committee needs to use its in-
         dustry and business understanding to
         determine whether the accounting esti-
         mates raised by management are reason-
         able. The audit committee also needs to
         get an understanding of these accounting
         estimates and management's justification
         for them.

         • Who has the authority to raise accounting
           estimates and what limited review

procedures have been put in place?

The audit committee needs to have an understanding as to whether these estimates were reviewed by a competent and qualified member of senior management.

- Is management adopting a conservative or aggressive accounting policy by raising the accounting estimates?

The raising of accounting estimates can either be aggressive or conservative and can have a significant effect on the reported results of an entity. The committee therefore needs to have an understanding of the effect of accounting estimates on the financial statements. The committee also needs to assess various assumptions underlying accounting estimates in financial statements.

### 5.2.3 *External audit*

- How did the external auditors gain sufficient and appropriate audit evidence to support the accounting estimates?
- A formalised control environment will not govern the processing of accounting estimates and the external auditors will have to substantively assess the

accounting estimates raised by management through an understanding of the business and discussions with management. The audit committee needs to have an understanding of the approach followed and the results obtained by the external auditors.

- What are the external auditor's conclusions on each of the significant accounting estimates processed?

The external auditors should critically assess the accounting estimates processed by management and reach a conclusion on the suitability of these estimates. The audit committee needs to obtain an understanding of the areas where the external auditors differed from management in interpreting the factors used to justify the accounting estimates.

- How do these accounting estimates compare with the accounting policies and norms adopted by the company?

6. *Current developments in auditing, accounting, reporting and taxation*

6.1    The audit committee provides assurance on the fair presentation of the financial statements and consequently needs to stay up to date and be aware of accounting, auditing and tax related issues affecting the company and the industry within which the company operates.

## 6.2 *Internal and external auditing*

- The audit committee must have reasonable assurance that the assurance providers have the necessary competencies and resources to perform their functions; that the assurance providers have performed their functions; and that they have been properly assessed by the audit committee.

## 6.3 *Accounting*

The audit committee needs to ask and consider the response to the following questions.

- Have we as audit committee members stayed up to date with developments in the accounting standards which apply to the company?
- Is the audit committee aware of the implication of new accounting standards on the accounting policies currently employed and the effect on the underlying financial results presented?

A vital step that an audit committee performs is to review the financial statements to ensure that they are reliable and understandable. If it is unable to interpret, apply and assess accounting standards adopted and pending, it will not be able to achieve its goal of assurance to the board of directors.

- Have we, as an audit committee, access to specialist expertise as and when deemed necessary?

The audit committee needs to put the necessary structures in place to ensure that it remains technically proficient.

- Have we asked the external auditor to brief us as committee members on any pending changes to the accounting standards?

The external auditors are accounting and auditing experts and need to be aware of all pending changes to accounting and auditing standards. The committee needs to request the external auditors to brief them on pending changes and their effect on the entity. In this regard the committee needs to enter into dialogue with the external auditors proactively.

## 6.4    *Taxation*

- What is the tax status of the company and any of its subsidiaries and is this adequately reflected in the financial statements?
- Is the company up to date with tax returns and assessments?
- Is management adopting a conservative or aggressive taxation approach?
- Are the company and the Revenue Services in dispute in regard to the treatment of any item and has this been adequately reflected in the financial statements?

The committee needs to assess whether the disclosure of all tax related issues is complete and appropriately reflected in the financial statements. The committee needs to have candid discussions with both management and the external auditors to identify any areas of dispute.

- Has an external tax adviser been briefed to advise on any pending changes to taxation laws?

## 7.    *External auditor's communication*

7.1    The external auditors are the independent

assurance providers to the shareholders of the company and reach an independent conclusion regarding the fairness of the financial statements presented. The audit committee needs to use the external auditors extensively to achieve its goal of recommending to the board financial statements for approval.

7.2    The audit committee could consider asking the following questions of the external auditors.

- What is the final audit opinion expressed on the financial statements and how comfortable are the external auditors with their opinion?

The external auditors will express either a modified or an unmodified opinion on the financial statements. The audit committee should enquire over any areas of concern and what matters were debated before the external auditors expressed their modified or unmodified opinion.

- In producing the final external audit report to the audit committee, the external auditors should report what items were omitted or amended at the specific request of management and why?

The external audit report will be reviewed by management. The audit committee should insist that any comment or response by management must be in writing and form part of the committee's pack.

- What are the areas where the external auditors were in direct dispute with management and how were these areas resolved?

The audit committee needs to understand all areas of dispute between the external auditors and management. The understanding is required to ensure that the best solution has been achieved and presented. These issues could be identified in a separate meeting if necessary.

- What is the nature and amount of the items reflected on the summary of unadjusted audit differences?

The committee should have an understanding of the nature of the items reflected on the summary of unadjusted audit differences. This understanding should be used to assess the reliability of the underlying financial statements.

- What are the details of all accounting

principles and policies applied by the entity for which there are acceptable alternative principles?

The committee should request that the external auditors report on how the accounting policies adopted by the entity affect transparency, understandability and usefulness of the underlying financial information. These discussions should be used by the audit committee to determine whether the accounting policies used by management present the financial information faithfully, consistently and reliably.

• Have the external auditors identified and considered the impact of all special financial structures used (e.g., special purpose vehicles)?

The committee should request the external auditors to comment on material special purpose entities in operation and when these were created. The committee should be aware of the following types of transactions which may not be adequately reflected in the accounting records:

• Off balance sheet finance and special purpose financing structures.

- Would some of these structures or transactions permit a conclusion to keep them off balance sheet and if so, the impact on adequate disclosure and fair presentation?
- Unusual transactions that affect ownership rights (such as leveraged recapitalisation or joint ventures).
- What are the details of transactions entered into with related parties that are not in the ordinary course of business and have these been adequately disclosed?

Examples of these kinds of related party transactions include compensation agreements, loans, related party leases, use of the company's assets, or employment of close relatives.

- What unusual arrangements and/or transactions did you identify during the completion of the audit?

Examples of unusual arrangements would include sale and leaseback of assets, self-insurance, etc. Such arrangements should be brought to the attention of the audit committee members to ensure that they understand how the financial reporting is being affected.

- What is your interpretation on the clarity and transparency of the financial statements prepared?

Management, the audit committee and the external auditors should discuss the clarity and transparency of the financial statements and disclosures, to ensure that they are complete, accurate and a fair reflection of the past performance of the company.

- What is your assessment of the quality of the earnings?

This would include, inter alia, concerns such as any use of provisions to smooth earnings, once-off adjustments, aggressive use of provisions, booking earnings too early and the sustainability of earnings as reported.

8.  *Compliance with the current regulatory environment; legal and statutory requirements*

8.1  The entity will be subject to numerous laws and regulations, some of which may be specific to the industry.

8.2  The audit committee should ask the following types of questions in this regard:

- Are we aware and is there an awareness in the company of the legal framework within which it operates?
- Have management and internal audit performed any procedures to provide assurance to the audit committee regarding compliance with the relevant legislation, and what were the results of these procedures?
- Are we and they satisfied that sufficient work has been performed during the period testing compliance by the company? It may be necessary to obtain assurance from the compliance officer, if such a function exits.
- Has there been sufficient access to any outside legal advice and if so, that advice?
- Are any areas of non-compliance, past and present, adequately reflected in the financial statements?

9.  *Professional advice*

Is there any aspect on which the audit committee reasonably believes it should obtain independent professional advice?

10.  *Conclusion*

All the above should assist audit committees

in their consideration and review of the financial statements. If implemented it should improve the quality of assurance furnished to the board.

# Appendix E: Qualitative Corporate Governance

*Intellectual honesty is the foundation*

*The pillars are fairness, accountability, responsibility and transparency*

*Processes must not be weapons of mass distraction*

*Define the purpose of the business, its value drivers and identify its stakeholders*

*Performance is the ultimate social & economic responsibility*

*Align processes with the best interests of the company*

*The company's stakeholders are its ultimate compliance officer*

*Identify the major risks and key performance indicators*

*Monitor management's performance against the board's strategic and business plans*

*Competent and efficient internal audit committee and independent external audit*

---

> GOOD FAITH – no conflict and intellectual honesty
> CARE – for the company's assets as if one's own
> SKILL – one's practised ability applied for the company
> DILIGENCE – study the facts and understand the issues

---

**FEAR**

**Q1:** Do I have any conflict?
> Duty of Good Faith

**Q2:** Do I have all the facts to enable me to make a decision?
> Duties of Care, Skill & Diligence

**Q3:** Is this a rational business decision based on all the facts?
> Duties of Care, Skill & Diligence

**Q4:** Is the decision in the best interests of the company?
> Duties of Good Faith, Care & Skill

**PRIDE**

**Q5:** Is the communication to stakeholders transparent?
> Duties of Care, Skill & Diligence

**Q6:** Will the decision result in the company being and being seen to be a decent citizen and as acting responsibly towards and responsively to its stakeholders?
> Duties of Care & Skill

**ARROGANCE**

**GREED**

**Q7:** Does this decision amount to good stewardship of the company's assets?
> Duties of Care, Skill & Diligence

**Q8:** Have I exercised intellectual honesty and naivety?
> Duties of Good Faith, Care & Skill

**Q9:** Have I understood the board pack and the discussion at the boardroom table?
> Duties of Care & Skill

**Q10:** Would the board be embarrassed if its decision and the process adopted to arrive at its decision appeared in a national newspaper?
> Duties of Care & Skill

**SLOTH**